IEUAN LL. GRIFFITHS

An Atlas of African Affairs

METHUEN
LONDON AND NEW YORK

First published in 1984 by
Methuen & Co. Ltd
11 New Fetter Lane,
London EC4P 4EE
Revised edition 1985
Published in the USA by
Methuen & Co.
in association with Methuen, Inc.
29 West 35th Street,
New York, NY 10001

Printed in Great Britain at the
University Press, Cambridge

British Library
Cataloguing in Publication Data
Griffiths, Ieuan Ll.
    An atlas of African affairs.
    1. Africa
    I. Title
    960   DT20

    ISBN 0-416-30940-2
    (University paperback 842)

Library of Congress
Cataloging in Publication Data
Griffiths, Ieuan Ll.
    An atlas of African affairs.
    Bibliography: p.
    Includes index.
    1. Africa—Maps.
    2. Africa—History—Maps.
    3. Africa—Politics and government—1960.
    I. Title.
    G2445.G7   1983   910′.6
    83-675796
    ISBN 0-416-30940-2 (pbk.)

Contents

List of abbreviations

AEF	*Afrique Equatoriale Française*
AOF	*Afrique Occidentale Française*
BADEA	Arab Bank for Economic Development in Africa
CAR	Central African Republic
CEAO	*Communauté Economique de l'Afrique de l'Ouest*
DTA	Democratic Turnhalle Alliance
dwt	dead weight tons
EAC	East African Community
ECA	Economic Commission for Africa
ECOWAS	Economic Community of West African States
ELF	Eritrean Liberation Front
EPLF	Eritrean People's Liberation Front
FAO	Food and Agriculture Organization
FNLA	*Frente Nacional de Libertacao de Angola*
FRELIMO	*Frente de Libertacao de Moçambique*
GDP	gross domestic product
GNP	gross national product
IMF	International Monetary Fund
ITCZ	inter-tropical convergence zone
LNG	liquefied natural gas
MNR	Mozambique National Resistance
MPLA	*Movimento Popular de Libertacao de Angola*
MRU	Mano River Union
NCO	non-commissioned officer
OAU	Organization of African Unity
OCAM	*Organization Commune Africaine et Mauricienne*
OPEC	Organisation of Petroleum Exporting Countries
POLISARIO	*Frente Popular para la Liberacion de Saguia el Hamra y Rio de Oro*
SACU	Southern African Customs Union
SADCC	Southern Africa Development Co-ordination Conference
SADR	Saharan Arab Democratic Republic
SUMED	Suez–Mediterranean oil pipeline
SWAPO	South West Africa People's Organization
TAZARA	Tanzania–Zambia Railway
UAR	United Arab Republic

UDEAC	*L'Union Douaniere et Economique de l'Afrique Centrale*
UDI	Unilateral declaration of independence
UN	United Nations
UNCTAD	United Nations Conference on Trade and Development
UNITA	*Uniao Nacional para a Independencia Total de Angola*
UPC	Uganda Peoples' Congress
US	United States (of America)
WHO	World Health Organization

Notes on maps

The maps of continental Africa are drawn on Lambert's Azimuthal Equal-Area Projection based on the Equator and the 20° East Meridian which are represented as straight lines.

Background information for maps 13 and 15 is from maps in J.S. Keltie (1893) *The Partition of Africa*, London, Stanford, p. 400; hence, for example, the name 'Erythrea'.

Mineral/mining symbols, wherever shown, are according to the key on map 40 (p. 127).

Maps drawn by Susan Rowland.

Preface

This book is very much the product of teaching and researching for many years in the stimulating inter-disciplinary environment of the School of African and Asian Studies at the University of Sussex. Fruitful hours were spent in the libraries of the University and the Institute of Development Studies. Above all the book owes most to warmly remembered years and months spent in Africa from the Cape to Cairo, from Las Palmas to Zanzibar. I am grateful to all who helped along the way.

Specifically I wish to thank Susan Rowland for drawing the maps so superbly and for patiently accommodating inevitable changes. Also Pat Bellamy for typing the manuscript. Don Funnell, Allan Potts and Tony Binns each read parts of the manuscript and offered valued comments. Final responsibility for errors of fact or judgement is mine but it was good to have had generous assistance from so many.

IEUAN LL. GRIFFITHS
University of Sussex
September 1983

A Environmental

1 Africa: barrier peninsula

Africa is completely surrounded by water except where it borders on Asia. The Egyptian king Necho was the first to establish this fact. After he desisted from trying to dig the canal that extends from the Nile to the Arabian Gulf, he sent some Phoenicians in ships with orders to sail back into the Mediterranean Sea by passing through the Pillars of Hercules and so return to Egypt. The Phoenicians left Egypt by way of the Red Sea and sailed into the southern ocean. When autumn came, they went ashore, wherever in Africa they were to sow grain and await the harvest. On reaping the grain they again set sail and thus after two years had passed they rounded the Pillars of Hercules and in the third year reached Egypt. They told a tale that I do not believe, though others may, that in sailing along the African coast they had the sun on their right hand.

(Herodotus *c.* 440 BC)

Herodotus' throw-away line, of course, is now the very basis for believing the whole story. The canal was duly completed in 521 BC by Darius the Persian. He marked its course with three rose granite *Stelae* which record: 'this canal was dug as I [Darius] commanded, and ships passed from Egypt through this canal to Persia as was my will.'

So the ancient world came to grips with one of the basic geographical problems posed by Africa, a vast barrier peninsula joined to the Eurasian landmass by the 100 mile (160 km) isthmus of Suez. Modern solutions to the problem are basically the same as the ancient. In AD 1498 Vasco da Gama circumnavigated Africa from west to east, and in AD 1869 a new Suez canal, this time direct to the Mediterranean, was at last completed by Ferdinand de Lesseps.

The African barrier is more formidable than the isthmus of Suez or the 10,000 mile (16,000 km) coastline. The Sahara desert, some 1500 miles (2400 km) across, completely spans the great northern width of Africa, severely limiting overland and even coastal communication. From the seventh century AD Islam spread across northern Africa bringing extensive cultural change and forming another barrier to wider contacts. The 'barrier' role applies to Africa today. Supertankers carrying oil from the Persian Gulf are too big to go through even the enlarged Suez canal and have to take the Cape sea route. During recent (post-1956) enforced closures of the canal *all* east–west maritime trade has had to make that long haul.

For black Africa the barriers have meant isolation that has never been

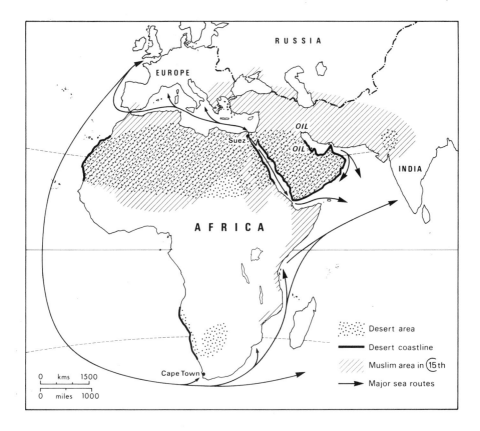

Desert area

Desert coastline

Muslim area in 15th

Major sea routes

complete but has been serious enough, for example, to account for the absence of the wheel. In this century of threatened nuclear catastrophe Africa's physical isolation could be its saving grace. A nuclear-free zone south of the Sahara might be a more desirable aim for black Africa than the nuclear stratagems urged on its richer countries by some political scientists. An imported, hideously expensive, high technology means of buying one's right to indulge in nuclear 'deterrence' seems to be an inappropriate way to acquire political influence especially when the freedom from such capability might ensure survival and so a safer path forward.

2 The physique of Africa

Africa straddles the equator, extending almost as far south as it does north. This simple geographical fact is of enormous significance as it is the basis for understanding the rather symmetrical distribution of African climates, vegetation and peoples. Notwithstanding their very different shapes and sizes, to a large extent the south is a mirror image of the north, the Kalahari matches the Sahara, the Karroo the Maghreb, and the Cape the Mediterranean littoral. At the centre is the equatorial forest of the Zaire (Congo) basin. To the north and north-east Africa is separated from Eurasia by narrow seas but is also joined to it by the isthmus of Suez. The adjacent location of Arabia, and beyond that Persia, means that north-eastern Africa is arid almost to the equator, an important exception to the symmetry along the line of the equator.

Africa comprises a single tectonic plate; though some would differentiate the area east of the Rift valley system. Almost the entire continent is a geologically stable land-mass of pre-Cambrian basement rocks overlain in part by later sedimentary cover. In the extreme south-west corner the Cape Fold Mountains are of Hercynian age, in the extreme north-west the Atlas Fold Mountains are of the Alpine orogeny. Elsewhere the stability is broken only by the great Rift Valley system.

In contrast to Europe the continent of Africa has a remarkably smooth outline. Its coastline is short relative to its area and there are few major inlets or peninsulas. On a smaller scale there is a marked absence of natural harbours. The continental shelf of Africa, again in contrast with Europe, is almost uniformly narrow. The major exception is in the south where the Agulhas Bank off the southern-most tip of Africa extends some 200 miles (320 km) off shore. The absence of a wide continental shelf limits fishing opportunities and reduces the chances of discovering major oilfields. Africa has relatively few offshore islands and most are small and of volcanic origin. The major exception is Madagascar, which ranks as the world's fourth largest subcontinental island.

The ocean currents off the African coast are influenced by the continental straddling of the equator. On the east coast the westward flowing North-Equatorial Current of the Indian Ocean divides to flow northwards as the Monsoon Drift and southwards as the Mozambique Current. The Monsoon Drift flows northwards in the northern summer but is reversed in the northern winter, historically a major factor in trading links between east Africa and Arabia, the Gulf and India. The Mozambique Current sweeps down the coast of south-eastern Africa as a swift warm current. On the west coast the currents flow

4

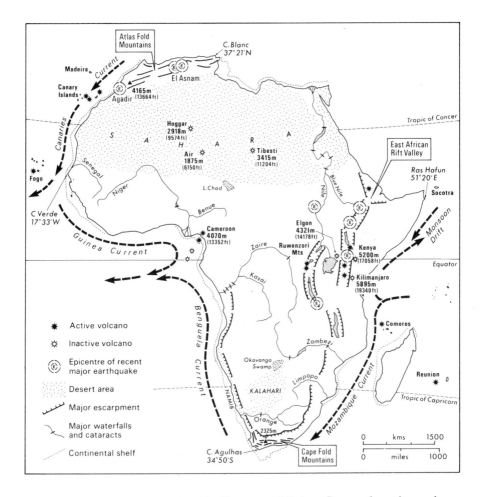

towards the equator as the Canaries Current and Guinea Current from the north and the Benguela Current from the south. They are cold currents, especially the fast-flowing Benguela. The Canaries Current and the Benguela Current flow for hundreds of miles along hot desert coasts well known for hazardous fogs caused by this juxtaposition.

Africa is a continent of wide horizons on broad, flat plateau surfaces. Plains cover thousands of square miles, stretching away, seemingly endless, in a featureless landscape. The plateau consists of a number of vast, shallow basins separated often by barely discernible watersheds, occasionally by mountainous tracts of considerable height as in the Tibesti, Aïr and Hoggar mountains of the Sahara. In southern Africa the Kalahari basin presents an outward-facing

5

scarped rim, the Great Escarpment, which in places rises to 10,000 feet (3000 m) proving a formidable obstacle to transport development.

The Cape Fold Mountains are wrapped, in a series of parallel ranges, around the south-west corner of the continent. They are aligned north–south along the west coast for about 150 miles (240 km) then swing through 90 degrees to run west–east along the south coast for over 600 miles (900 km). The ranges are steep and high, reaching 7632 feet (2325 m), with literally dozens of peaks of over 5000 feet (1500 m). The Cape Mountains make for spectacular scenery especially near the coast, as in the Cape Peninsula, but also in the narrow gorges (*poorts*) cut through the ranges. Being near to the coast and roughly parallel with it throughout their length the Cape Fold Mountains were a most effective barrier to penetration of the continental interior by man and by rain-bearing winds.

The Atlas Mountains occupy the north-western corner of Africa and are an extension of the Alpine system of Europe. Consisting of a number of roughly parallel ranges with intermontane plateaux and valleys they extend in a belt up to 200 miles (320 km) wide from Tunisia to southern Morocco, a distance of 1400 miles (2250 km). Seldom above 5000 feet (1500 m) in Tunisia, there are two main ranges in Algeria divided by a plateau. In Morocco there are four main ranges, the Rif, Middle, High and Anti Atlas and it is in the High Atlas that the greatest elevation of 13,664 feet (4165 m) is attained, far higher than the older Cape Mountains. The Atlas Mountains are parallel with the northern coastline of the Maghreb and so cut off the north-western Sahara from maritime influence.

The ancient surfaces of Africa are disrupted on the eastern side of the continent by the great Rift Valley system which extends roughly north–south from the Red Sea to the Zambezi (and northwards along the Red Sea to the Dead Sea and the Jordan valley). From the Red Sea the Rift Valley cuts through the Ethiopian highlands; in east Africa there are two Rift Valleys, eastern and western, which unite in the southern or Malawi section. The rifts are prominent features in the landscape, great trenches 20–50 miles (30–80 km) wide, with inward-facing walls, sometimes very steep, sometimes stepped, themselves up to 3000 feet (1000 m) high, an unmistakable and unforgettable sight.

The east African rifts have closely associated volcanic and seismic activity and many of the active volcanoes of Africa are to be found here, some towering on the valley sides, some actually on the rift floor. Near the eastern edge of the eastern rift are the two highest mountains in Africa, Kilimanjaro (19,340 ft, 5895 m) and Kenya (17,058 ft, 5200 m), both inactive volcanoes. The Rift Valley areas experience frequent earth tremors and occasional large earthquakes including the largest in Africa this century, near the southern end of Lake Tanganyika in the western rift. Other earthquake-prone areas in Africa include the Atlas Mountains where recently there has been considerable loss of life at Agadir and twice at El Asnam. Africa's largest active volcano is Mount Cameroon (13,352 ft,

4070 m) which is part of a chain of volcanoes which stretches far out to sea. It is recorded that when the Portuguese first sailed into these waters in the fifteenth century and saw on either side towering volcanoes belching smoke and fire they turned and fled convinced they had found the very Gates of Hell. Africa's other active volcanoes are on the offshore islands, notably the Canaries, where, in a less religious age, they are now a major tourist attraction well worth a visit.

Also associated with the Rift Valley system are the great lakes of east Africa. In the Rift Valley floors they are characteristically long, narrow and sometimes of great depth; on the plateau between the rifts lies the relatively broad and shallow Lake Victoria, the third largest lake in the world. In the Lake Victoria basin is the long-sought-after source of the Nile, reputedly the longest river in the world (4150 miles, 6640 km). While almost one-third of Africa is desert, another third is drained by five great rivers, the Nile, Zaire (Congo), Niger, Zambezi and Orange. Because of the plateau basin structure of the African interior none of the major rivers is navigable inland from the sea for any great distance, in contrast to the great rivers of the Americas and Europe. The Nile is navigable 960 miles (1500 km) to Aswan, the Zaire 150 miles (240 km) to Matadi, the Niger 120 miles (200 km) to Onitsha all the year round, the Zambezi is open only to shallow-draught boats to Tete 300 miles (500 km) from the mouth, while the Orange is simply not navigable. The Nile, Zaire and Niger do have long navigable interior stretches but they are also broken by further falls and cataracts. The Zaire has the most extensive inland waterway system with the greatest single stretch from Kinshasa to Kisangani, about 1090 miles (1740 km) in Conrad's 'heart of darkness'. The absence of navigable waterways from the sea kept explorers, traders and colonizers at bay and it is an impediment to economic development except that such disadvantage is considerably outweighed by the enormous hydroelectricity potential being realized on all the major rivers at points where they plunge over the basin rims and escarpments.

The physique of Africa is very different from that of any other continent. Its unique characteristics have done much to shape the lives of its peoples and provide it with enormous potential for future development.

3 Sunshine and storm

Rainfall is the climatic factor of greatest significance in Africa. Most of the continent has a small annual range of temperature, and wind is also much less of a feature than in temperate latitudes. Africa extends little beyond 35 degrees of latitude from the equator. This limits the range of African climates and also means that the basic movement of air over most of the continent is towards the equator, or more accurately, towards the inter-tropical convergence zone (ITCZ). The actual position of the ITCZ shifts with the seasonal movement of the sun across the tropics. In July the ITCZ lies across north Africa along the southern edge of the Sahara; in January it skirts the west African coast, snakes along the northern and eastern margins of the Zaire (Congo) basin and thence over Madagascar. The ITCZ influences the distribution of climatic zones which assume some symmetry about the equator as Africa extends almost as far south as it does north of the line. That symmetry is distorted by the effect of the adjacent Eurasian land-mass and by highland areas within Africa.

The climatic zones of Africa are shown according to Thornthwaite's classification. Largely because only the two warmest of the six temperature efficiency classes are present, Africa has only nineteen different climatic zones, most of which are found in more than one part of the continent.

Thornthwaite's classification

I	Precipitation effectiveness	2	Temperature efficiency	3	Seasonal rainfall
A	Wet	A′	Tropical	v	adequate all seasons
B	Humid	B′	Mesothermal	s	deficient in summer
C	Sub-humid	*C′	Microthermal	w	deficient in winter
D	Semi-arid	*D′	Taiga	d	deficient all seasons
E	Arid	*E′	Tundra		
		*F′	Frost		

* Not represented in Africa

The wet tropical climates (AA′v) in Africa are limited to the coastal strips of Sierra Leone/Liberia, the Nigeria/Cameroon border, and eastern Madagascar. These areas experience rain at all seasons with an annual average of up to 200 inches (5000 mm), and mean annual temperatures of about 79°F (26°C) with an annual range of only 4°F (2°C).

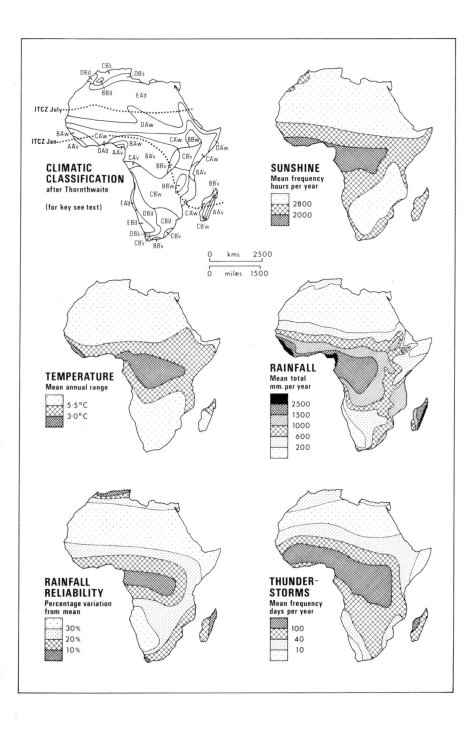

CLIMATIC CLASSIFICATION
after Thornthwaite

(for key see text)

CB's
DB'd
DB's
BB'd
EA'd
ITCZ July
DA'w
BA'w
CA'w
ITCZ Jan
BA'v
CA'w
BB'w
AA'v
DA'w
AA'v
DA'd
AA'v
BA'v
CA'w
CA'v
BA'v
CB'v
BB'v
BA'v
BB'w
BB'v
EA'd
DB'd
CB'd
CA'w
AA'v
EB'd
CB'w
DB's
CB'v
CB's
BB'v

0   kms   2500
0   miles   1500

SUNSHINE
Mean frequency
hours per year

2800
2000

TEMPERATURE
Mean annual range

5·5°C
3·0°C

RAINFALL
Mean total
mm. per year

2500
1500
1000
600
200

**RAINFALL
RELIABILITY**
Percentage variation
from mean

30%
20%
10%

**THUNDER-
STORMS**
Mean frequency
days per year

100
40
10

Inland, rainfall decreases with a drier winter season (BA'w). The Zaire (Congo) basin is surprisingly dry for an equatorial lowland with a seasonally well-distributed mean annual rainfall of 40–80 inches (1000–2000 mm), mean annual temperatures of 68°–77°F (20°–25°C), low annual temperature range, and high humidity (BA'v). A similar climate is found on the Kenyan and north Tanzanian coasts. The mountains of Rwanda, Burundi and the Ruwenzoris, the mountain core of Madagascar, and the Tsitsikama mountains on the southern coast of the Cape Province of South Africa, all have a similar climate modified by elevation and latitude (BB'v) with an annual rainfall of up to 100 inches (2500 mm) but lower mean annual temperatures of about 60°F (16°C). The Ethiopian highlands and the highlands of south-western Tanzania/Malawi also have a similar climate but with a dry winter season (BB'w) with lower annual rainfall totals and lower mean annual temperatures with frost experienced at higher altitudes.

The sub-humid climates of Africa mainly extend in an arc around the wet and humid equatorial core, but also are found beyond the arid zones at the northern and southern extremities of the continent. The sub-humid, tropical dry winter season belt (CA'w) stretches across Africa from Senegal to Somalia and also appears in northern Mozambique and Madagascar. Annual rainfall is typically 30–40 inches (750–1000 mm), and mean annual temperatures are higher than in the humid zone. Further from the equator the dry winter season becomes longer and more pronounced. In east Africa both elevation and the local influence of Lake Victoria modify the climate with lower mean annual temperatures and a less marked dry season (CB'v). A similar climate is experienced in Natal. The interior of southern Africa is similar to but cooler than the Sudanic belt (CB'w), and over much of south Africa rainfall is deficient in all seasons (CB'd). In the western Cape and the coastal Maghreb is a Mediterranean-type climate of warm, dry summers and cool, wet winters (CB's) with annual rainfall of 30 inches (750 mm) or less, about two-thirds falling in the four winter months.

The semi-arid climates border the Sahara, hence the name Sahel (border) for the narrow belt of prolonged dry winter season climate (DA'w) which extends right across northern Africa. It has an annual rainfall of under 20 inches (500 mm), and high temperatures with a high diurnal range. In southern Africa the semi-desert, which takes in much of the Kalahari, is cooler, and deficient of rain in all seasons (DB'd). Between the deserts and the Mediterranean zones areas of semi-arid climate are found with summer rainfall deficiency (DB's).

The arid zone of the Sahara desert (EA'd) covers about 30 per cent of the continent. It is dry with extremely low, erratic rainfall, high sunshine values of up to 98 per cent, very high temperatures, including the highest ever recorded at Azizia, Libya (136.4°F, 57.7°C), and very high diurnal range of temperature. The counterpart in southern Africa, the narrow Namib desert, extends along the coast of Namibia. Its southern extension is rather cooler (EB′d) because of latitude and the fogs caused by the cold Benguela Current.

The selected characteristics of African climate illustrated all show, with varied detail, the essential onion-like pattern of climatic zones: from the cloudy, warm, wet, monotonously uniform, thunderstormed core, layer upon layer to the sunny, hot, dry desert-skin.

Africa really is the continent of sunshine and storm. In the eastern Sahara a wide area experiences in excess of 4000 hours of sunshine a year (over 91 per cent of possible sunshine), in Kampala there are, on average, 242 days a year with thunderstorms. Who can forget stepping on to the tarmac at Entebbe to feel the intense heat of the equatorial sun, and then in the Kampala afternoon the lashing rain, flashing lightning and frightening thunder of the suddenly unleashed tropical storm, followed by the cool fragrant evening on Makerere Hill? Or when sailing in air-conditioned comfort up the Red Sea, the breath-taking blast of heat as you go on deck, or when driving through the pounding hailstones of Kericho anxious for the haven of the Tea Hotel, or the Berg wind in February searing down on Durban at 104°F (40°C), or just waiting for a few hot, humid hours in the *old* customs shed at Lagos airport. Such are the lasting impressions of African climate.

Climatic conditions in many parts of Africa are trying for humans. The monotony of heat, humidity and daily 'climatic' regime in humid, tropical areas is profoundly enervating. Great stress is imposed by oppressive heat as along the southern Red Sea coast and the Somali interior. Then there are the indirect effects of climate in disease and pestilence, drought and famine, flood and devastation. On the other hand the sunshine, warmth and refreshing rains make so much of Africa a delightful environment.

4 Soils

The soils of Africa most favourable to human occupance are found in the major river valleys whose rich alluvial deposits have been worked for centuries or, in the case of the Nile, millennia. With few exceptions, elsewhere the soils of Africa are difficult and while improvement can be made to husband natural fertility, the basic raw materials and the climatic environment conspire against such progress.

African soils are highly varied and even the most detailed maps available on a continental scale have vast areas marked 'undifferentiated' or are a mosaic of difficult-to-generalize detail. The limitations of a small-scale map of African soils are almost total. The most one can hope to do is draw attention to the close relationship between climate and soils by showing that the broad pattern of soil distribution bears some resemblance to generalized climatic zones.

The wet and humid tropical areas have deep soils built up by the intense activity of biological and chemical processes stimulated by heat and moisture. The soils are protected against erosion by the thick forest cover itself, the rapid decomposition (and renewal) of which aids a steady supply of organic material to the upper soil layers. Unfortunately this process is no match for the high rainfall which leaches out of the soil most of the plant nutrients leaving low-fertility, difficult soils, often with a hard pan formed of iron or aluminium oxides. These difficult soils are known as *latosols* or *ferrosols*, the best known of which is laterite. There are some areas of better soils in the wet tropics as in southern Nigeria but they are of limited extent. Much needs to be learned about tropical soils so that they might be utilized to best advantage. Massive problems of soil erosion can occur where the forest cover has been cleared on a large scale.

The areas between the wet tropics and the deserts match their transitional climates and transitional vegetations with transitional soils. Nearest the latosols are the *luvisols*, well-developed soils, locally rich in plant nutrients but often with iron-oxide hard pan making agriculture difficult. Towards the deserts *arenosols*, sandy soils, often deep but low in humus content and not very fertile, predominate, giving way in turn to *xerosols* which have a very low humus content over sands and gravels.

In south-western Africa the area of Kalahari sand extends northwards in a great swathe through Botswana, Namibia, western Zambia, Angola and into Zaire. Soils in this area are arenosols, deep but low in humus content and easily broken down into a not very productive sandy tilth. Riding even very wide-tyred bicycles in Ovamboland or driving low-slung cars in Zambia's Kafue National Park are hazardous occupations in this sand, and once experienced are for ever to

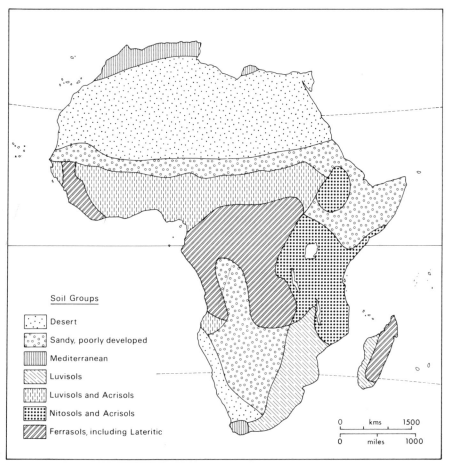

Soil Groups

- ⋱ Desert
- ° ° ° Sandy, poorly developed
- Mediterranean
- Luvisols
- Luvisols and Acrisols
- Nitosols and Acrisols
- Ferrasols, including Lateritic

0   kms   1500
0   miles   1000

be avoided. To eke a living out of such soils is extremely difficult. The only soils which are more difficult are the true desert soils which include xerosols, *yermosols* and simply blown sand or bare rock.

The soils of Africa are a poor resource that is likely to deteriorate dramatically under pressure from increasing populations. Over much of the continent soil erosion is already a major problem. On a continent where the vast majority of people live directly off the land the consequences of further deterioration could be serious to the point of catastrophic.

13

5 Vegetation

The familiar distributional pattern of concentric arcs around the Zaire (Congo) basin derives from the close relationship between natural vegetation and climate although there are some important local/regional variations due to soils, drainage and elevation. There are, in fact, very few areas of Africa where the 'natural' vegetation has not been strongly modified by human cultivation, herding and hunting. Population growth in Africa is rapidly increasing man's impact on the vegetational environment.

At the centre of the continent is the tropical rain forest. Developed on lowlands with year-round precipitation it extends throughout the Zaire (Congo) basin and along the west African coast where the forest belt is widest in Sierra Leone. Forest also extends in a very narrow belt along the south-eastern coast south from the equator. In Madagascar there is a rather different form of rain forest with several species not known on the African mainland. The rain forest is florally rich with numerous species of trees, shrubs, ferns and mosses. The forest floor is dark under a double or triple canopy of trees. Stands of individual species are rare, so economic exploitation of the forest, in its natural state, is difficult.

Man's activities are destroying vast areas of tropical rain forest in Africa. Clearing for agriculture, fuel wood, charcoal or construction timber has become all too easy in the age of the chain-saw and bulldozer. The effects can be harmful where no replanting takes place. In the short term there are often serious soil erosion problems as well as the possible destruction of entire plant species. In the long term the effects of wholesale forest clearance on local and even world climates is a matter of serious scientific concern.

The margin of the rain forest coincides with the development of a dry winter season. In such areas there is often a mosaic of forest and savanna. Further away from the forest, as the dry season becomes more pronounced and more prolonged the savanna woodland thins out and more drought-resistant tree species are found. The savanna is the land of big game in Africa but it is also disease-ridden and in general does not support high densities of population because of its climate and soils.

Further still from the equator the savanna degenerates into semi-arid and then desert. This is the environment of the Sahel, ranging from thorn-wooded grassland to tussocky grasses with large patches of bare earth between. The semi-arid areas are overpopulated by humans and animals and both take their toll on the environment. As pasture is destroyed through over-grazing the desert

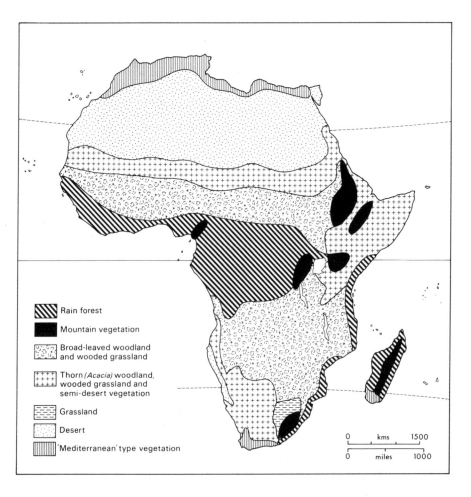

Rain forest

Mountain vegetation

Broad-leaved woodland and wooded grassland

Thorn *(Acacia)* woodland, wooded grassland and semi-desert vegetation

Grassland

Desert

'Mediterranean' type vegetation

| 0 | kms | 1500 |
| 0 | miles | 1000 |

advances relentlessly southwards further restricting populations and increasing densities in a vicious circle of desertification.

Beyond the deserts is the Mediterranean-type vegetation of north and south, drought-resistant, *maquis*-like vegetation capable of withstanding the warm dry summers. In the Cape the flora is quite distinctive but unique indigenous plants such as the protea have to fight for survival with introduced exotics.

Conservation in Africa needs to ensure that the often appalling immediate pressures do not result in short-term solutions which are themselves destructive in the longer term. There are too many new Sahelian water boreholes which have simply led to the destruction of all vegetation within a wide radius.

6 Drought and famine

Drought and famine are endemic in the semi-arid areas of Africa on the desert fringes. The Sahel, or the southern margin of the Sahara desert; the lands surrounding the Ethiopian highlands and large parts of southern Africa have all suffered severe cyclical drought in recent years. They are areas where, at best, man makes a precarious living. In the early 1970s tens of thousands of people died of starvation in the Sahel and Ethiopia because of severe drought throughout the area. That crisis continued until after the return of normal rains in late 1974. Since then rainfall has been below average levels though not at crisis point. In 1980 the same lethal combination of drought, famine and starvation swept through lands marginal to the Ethiopian highlands. The Karamoja district of north-eastern Uganda and the Ogaden in Ethiopia and Somalia were the worst hit areas and again thousands of people died. In 1983–5 northern Ethiopia was devastated by severe drought. Thousands died before effective international emergency aid was mobilized. Southern Africa, too, has been subjected to severe cyclical droughts; the latest, in 1983, affecting large parts of South Africa, Botswana, Zimbabwe and Zambia. In these recurrent crises not only do people suffer and die but the future viability of the local economies is undermined by wholesale destruction of livestock herds.

Rainfall in the marginal lands is low and unreliable. Average rainfall is less than 24 inches (600 mm) per annum, falling in a single, short, rainy season. Rainfall is unpredictable in amount and timing; the smaller the average rainfall the less the reliability. In the early 1970s the drier lands in the Sahel were more adversely affected than the wetter. The nearer the Sahara the greater the average rainfall deficiency against the local norm. High temperatures and high sunshine rates severely reduce rainfall effectiveness.

All the drought-stricken areas are apparently subject to long-term cyclic variations in rainfall. In this century the Sahel has experienced severe droughts at approximately thirty-year intervals. The median years of the dry periods were 1913, 1942 and 1971, when respectively 59 per cent, 79 per cent and 70 per cent of 'normal' rainfall was experienced. In each of these dry periods drought conditions prevailed for a number of successive years. Over the five years 1968–1972 rainfall averaged only 81 per cent of the norm creating a cumulative effect of rainfall deficiency more serious than in the two other dry periods of this century. This drought was preceded by above average rainfall throughout the 1950s and early 1960s which created greater problems, for in the wetter years population and livestock numbers multiplied.

16

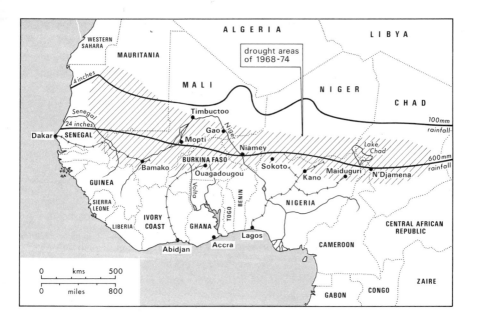

The population increase was part of a longer term trend which even in the sparsely populated Sahelian countries amounted to a population explosion. Births at 45–50 per thousand were roughly double the deaths at 20–25 per thousand, because of better health care and improved nutritional standards. The drought surprisingly did not have much visible effect on birth- and death-rates although the former did fall in the 1970–5 period. But the meagre and dwindling resources of the Sahel in the drought had to be shared by many more people; there were simply many more mouths to feed than in the past.

In such a crisis the first major problem is the delay in implementing effective aid because time inevitably elapses before a crisis is even recognized. More time is taken to realize that it is beyond the capabilities of an individual state. Yet more time is needed to alert and convince international agencies that there is a crisis of such magnitude that it really does require co-ordinated international aid. Even more time is taken to work out the complicated logistics of getting the right sort of assistance to where it is needed, and finally time is needed actually to carry out the operation. Delay can have a critical effect not only on the immediate human suffering and loss of life but also on the duration of the crisis. Destruction of the seed-corn or, in the case of these arid lands, the decimation of the livestock herds have devastating long-term effects.

Gaining access to the needy in the arid lands is not easy. Population is sparse, fewer than twelve persons per square mile (five per sq. km) over millions of

17

square miles. The easiest way to give out aid is to concentrate the people at distribution points, which quickly become refugee camps for people drawn from vast areas. These large concentrations of people create their own problems in areas which, even in normal climatic years, are far too dry to support such a high density of population. Water supply is critical but simply crowding people together in dry, dusty conditions immediately creates sanitation and health problems. Shelter has to be provided against the cold nights and hot days. What may have started as a 'simple' matter of food supply soon escalates into a major, multifaceted and very expensive relief operation.

The logistics of moving large amounts of food into the Sahel were extremely difficult. Modern transport access was severely limited. The drought areas were served by very few railways, from Dakar to Bamako and then on to the navigable Niger; from Abidjan to Ouagadougou; and in the east the three northern termini of Nigerian railways at Kaura Namoda, Nguru and Maiduguri. All the railways terminate in the least-affected southern fringe of the Sahel whence distribution of supplies had to be made by road. At the time of the drought the only tarred roads to penetrate the Sahel from the coast were from Accra to Ouagadougou and from Lagos via Sokoto to the Niger border and via Kano into southern Niger. Within the Sahel a tarred road connected Bamako and Mopti, while around Niamey the road along the Niger valley was tarred for about 250 miles (400 km). Most were on the southern fringe of the drought-stricken area. Up-country roads in the Sahel were (and are) mainly ungraded tracks of poor quality and it was over these that the much-needed supplies had to be carried in lorries and four-wheel-drive vehicles. Within the Sahel, Bamako and Kano were the only major airports, but about twenty other airports had scheduled flights, mainly by small aircraft, DC3s or smaller. In the emergency Hercules transport aircraft were used to fly food and medical supplies to these airports and to many improvised airstrips.

Distances to and within the Sahel are vast. From Accra to Ouagadougou by road is 625 miles (1000 km), from Dakar to Bamako by rail is over 800 miles (1300 km). Within Mali, from Bamako to Gao is 750 miles (1200 km) by road, only half the distance being tarred. Within Niger, from Niamey to the tip of Lake Chad is 940 miles (1500 km) by road, of which less than 200 miles (320 km) was tarred in the early 1970s.

In the arid land around the Ethiopian highlands, natural disaster has been compounded by wars and international politics. In the Ogaden the Somali/Ethiopian conflict of 1978–9 coincided with widespread drought. In Karamoja the age-old cross-border cattle wars were intensified as modern weaponry became available following the rout of Amin's forces in 1979. Famine relief in remote parts of Uganda became not only extremely difficult but positively dangerous, forcing aid organizations periodically to suspend operations because of danger to personnel.

The Ethiopian droughts of 1983–5 mainly affected Tigre and Eritrea where protracted war helped cause famine, added to human suffering and made relief access difficult. The Ethiopian government gave prosecution of war priority over famine relief. It was reluctant to accept western military aid to help solve the logistics of famine relief and even gave priority to Soviet arms ships over grain ships at the port of Assab. It denied suggestions that its ideologically-bound agricultural policy was a root cause of the crisis and that lavish celebrations marking the tenth anniversary of its coming to power were, in the circumstances, grotesque. The Soviet Union did little to help and almost nothing until after western intervention. Western powers were slow to respond and it took a harrowing BBC-TV report in October 1984 to shock the west into sending emergency food aid. Caught in a web of callous political manoeuvre tens of thousands died of starvation unnecessarily. Cyclical drought was a remote factor in this most human tragedy.

The long-term prospects are grim. Periodic drought is a fact of life in the semi-arid areas. Continued population increase puts pressure on the land. As population and livestock densities increase so does vulnerability to the inevitable periodic drought. Funds are not a problem now, almost the reverse. Through such organizations as the *Club des Amis du Sahel* vast amounts of long-term aid have been poured into the Sahelian countries and through the careful monitoring of the Emergency Service of the World Food Programme no one need actually die of starvation except for human error or neglect. Not all the aid has been well spent but lessons have been learned. There is now a general acceptance among western field workers that indigenous agriculture is much more sophisticated and finely attuned to the problems posed by the local natural environment and its vagaries than had been previously appreciated. The need for co-ordination between the various agencies is now acknowledged. The point that an improvement here can actually cause a problem there is taken. Provision of a costly borehole can lead to land for a wide radius being trampled into barren uselessness by livestock brought to water. There is still a tendency to indulge in over-grand and/or totally inappropriate schemes based on 'expertise' from other continents and transferred without regard to physical and cultural differences. The balance of forces which allowed centuries of occupance of the dry lands has been irrevocably upset because it depended on periodic famine, appalling human suffering, everyday hardship and standards of health and well-being which are no longer acceptable. To make the harsh environment of the marginal dry lands a habitat where people can live materially better lives than in the past is a daunting challenge which is far from being met.

7 Disease and pestilence

Africa's climates encourage harmful insects, its water-supply problems interact with sanitation and hygiene, its poverty causes malnutrition. Many die from endemic diseases but many more are chronically sick from debilitating diseases which impair efficiency and lower the quality of life. In 1981 all tropical Africa plus the densely populated lower Nile valley and delta was malarial. Malaria is transmitted by some mosquitoes, for example, *Anopheles gambiae*. The World Health Organization (WHO) estimates 250 million people in Africa are exposed to the disease and about 'one million infants and children die each year'. Malaria is combated by draining swamps and pools, the breeding areas of the mosquito, and spraying with DDT, itself dangerous and destructive, costly and sometimes ineffective.

Yellow fever, a deadly disease also transmitted by mosquitoes, for example, *Aedes aegypti* and *A. africanus*, has been effectively controlled by vaccination and insecticides. But in tropical Africa epidemics still occur among populations not recently exposed to the virus. In 1982 eight African states reported infected areas. In the same way cholera and plague are still endemic to Africa. In 1982 fourteen states reported cholera-infected areas and three, Madagascar, Tanzania and Zimbabwe, plague. Numbers now affected by these diseases are small but they do emphasize the difficulty of complete eradication. River blindness (*Onchoceriasis*), transmitted by the small fly *Simulium damnosum*, has endemic foci in most of tropical Africa. In the savanna areas of west Africa alone WHO estimates more than 1 million people affected. Bilharzia (*Schistosomiasis*) is caused by a blood fluke hosted by a fresh-water snail picked up by drinking, bathing or washing in infected water. New irrigation schemes have resulted in new foci of infestation. 'Both human and animal *Trypanosomiasis* (sleeping sickness) are one of the serious obstacles to socioeconomic development.' About 35 million Africans are at risk from the disease transmitted by the tsetse fly. Its effect on cattle severely limits agricultural progress. The desert locust is a major pest in north Africa and the Horn. Its depredations often mean the difference between life and death in areas already stricken by drought. Tuberculosis and poliomyelitis, largely eliminated in the developed world, are widely prevalent in Africa, not least in urban slums.

Progress in disease control, largely a function of resources committed, has been made in recent years but much remains to be done before Africa is freed from the debilitating effects of its many endemic diseases. Fighting disease is a vital part of the fight against poverty and deprivation.

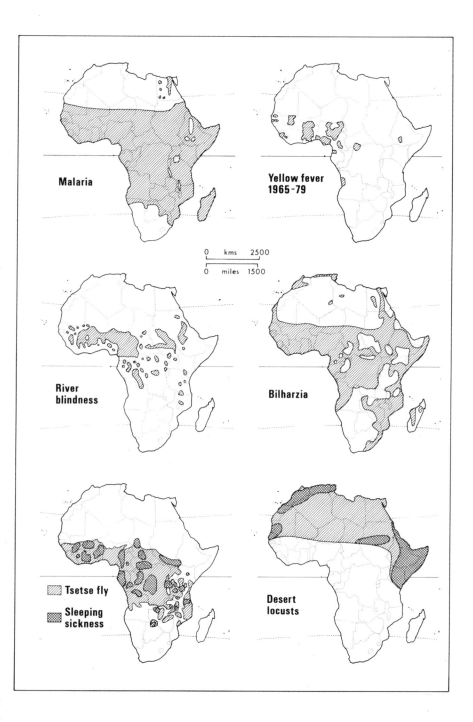

Malaria

Yellow fever
1965-79

River
blindness

Bilharzia

Tsetse fly
Sleeping
sickness

Desert
locusts

0   kms   2500
0   miles   1500

8 Population

The total population of Africa, by United Nations (UN) estimates, probably exceeds 500 million. The continent has an average population density of about 42 persons per square mile (16 per sq. km) compared with that of India of about 550 per square mile (200 per sq. km) but African population growth rates are now among the highest in the world.

Average figures convey little because distribution is far from uniform. Three vast areas, the Sahara desert, the Kalahari and Namib deserts, and the tropical rain forest of the Zaire (Congo) basin, support very small populations for obvious reasons. On the other hand, such areas as the lower Nile valley and delta of Egypt and the Mediterranean coastal belt of the Maghreb each have populations of about 40 million at high density. South of the Sahara the greatest concentration of population, over 50 million, is inland from the Gulf of Guinea from Ivory Coast to Cameroon. The fertile highlands of Rwanda and Burundi extending into the Kigezi province of Uganda support some of the highest densities of rural population on the continent, about 400 persons per square mile (150 per sq. km). The northern littoral of Lake Victoria from Buganda and Busoga to the Nyanza district of Kenya also supports a high density of rural population, as does southern Malawi and eastern South Africa from Zululand to the Ciskei. The high concentrations of urban population on the Zaire/Zambia copperbelt and the southern Transvaal mining and industrial complex also show up.

In some areas of high-density rural population severe pressure on the land is relieved by out-migration. From Rwanda, Burundi and Kigezi people move northwards extending intensive cultivation into the Ugandan provinces of Ankole and Toro. From the overpopulated South African 'homelands' people move to the towns in the migrant labour system. As African populations increase, pressure on land becomes more widespread, more people are forced to move and the related problems multiply, as in Kenya.

The population of Africa is growing rapidly, at an average rate of over 3 per cent per annum which, if continued, would see it doubled by the end of the century to about 1000 million. There are exceptionally high birth-rates and high, but declining, death-rates. Infant mortality is very high because of diseases such as malaria and measles and also because poor nutritional standards lower resistance to disease in general. Life expectancy is low but, in accord with the decreasing death-rate, is rising. Population is already a major problem in parts of Africa and is likely to become a more widespread one.

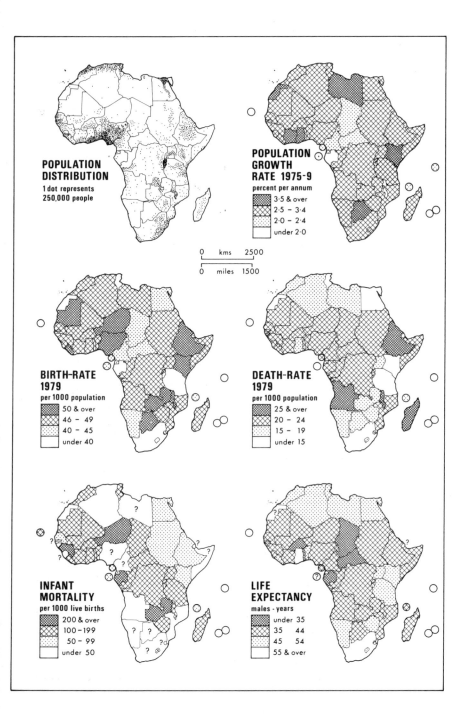

POPULATION DISTRIBUTION

1 dot represents 250,000 people

POPULATION GROWTH RATE 1975-9

percent per annum
- 3·5 & over
- 2·5 – 3·4
- 2·0 – 2·4
- under 2·0

BIRTH-RATE 1979

per 1000 population
- 50 & over
- 46 – 49
- 40 – 45
- under 40

DEATH-RATE 1979

per 1000 population
- 25 & over
- 20 – 24
- 15 – 19
- under 15

INFANT MORTALITY

per 1000 live births
- 200 & over
- 100 – 199
- 50 – 99
- under 50

LIFE EXPECTANCY

males – years
- under 35
- 35 44
- 45 54
- 55 & over

0 kms 2500

0 miles 1500

9 Languages

Two thousand different languages have been identified in Africa, some localized, some dialects of a family of languages, others widely spoken regional languages of trade. The distribution of languages is complex with many areas of linguistic overlap and, at any one place, 'layers' of language, each fulfilling a particular purpose. African facility in handling different languages is remarkable. The barely literate house-servant at Makerere would speak to her family in RuToro, to her neighbours in Luganda, to the traders in Swahili, to her employers in English and to her employers' amazement and near-monoglot embarrassment, to a visitor in fluent French, explaining that her former husband was Rwandaise.

The distribution of African languages bears no relationship to modern political boundaries and single language groups are often divided between two or more states. The peoples of Nigeria between them speak literally hundreds of different languages. The creation of national unity without a unifying language is difficult, and most states fall back on the former colonial language or an Africanized form of it.

Some states have a major local language as the official language. Swahili, the trading language of the east African coast, is the official language of Tanzania although it is not the hearth language of most Tanzanians. In making Somali their official language Somalia had to overcome the 'little' problem of standardizing a written form of the language. Other countries use a local language officially alongside the former colonial language. For black South Africans Afrikaans is the language of oppression and other African languages are the tools of the divide and rule homelands policy. Urban Blacks demand to be educated in English and in 1976 were prepared to die for that in Soweto.

African languages are classified into five basic groups. The *Khoisan* languages of the San (Bushmen) and Khoi-Khoi (Hottentots) are limited to the Kalahari where those peoples have sought survival under pressure from stronger Bantu and European language groups. Limited to the island of Madagascar the dialects of *Malagasy* are related to Indonesian. That stimulates speculation about Kon-Tiki-like migrations across the Indian Ocean on the westward-flowing equatorial currents. The *Afro-Asiatic* languages, chief of which is Arabic, are limited to Islamic Africa plus non-Islamic (traditionally Christian) Ethiopia where the official language is Amharic. The *Bantu* languages are the most widely distributed. They contain several individual families of languages such as the Nguni of south-eastern Africa which includes Xhosa, Zulu and Swazi. Some trading languages such as Fula are found at widely separated locations, others

Afro-Asiatic
(Hamito-Semitic)

Nilo-Saharan
(East Saharan)

Bantu
(Niger-Kordofarian)

Khoisan
(Bushmen-Hottentots)

Malayo-Polynesian
(Malagasy)

like Lingala are spoken over a single vast area. Between the two largest groups the *Nilo-Saharan* languages are found mainly in a great arc from northern Chad, to the southern Sudan, Uganda and western Kenya.

The preservation of African languages is not yet a problem but with increasing mobility and communication it could become a cultural issue. More than forty African languages are each spoken by more than 1 million people and they are vital to modern Africa. One of them, Wolof, demonstrates just that in fulfilling a major post-colonial task in helping to unite the peoples of Senegambia despite their different colonial experiences.

10 Literacy

In July 1966 an impressive ceremony was held in Lusaka to install the first chancellor of the University of Zambia. In the course of a long speech, the chancellor, President Kaunda, publicly wept for the educational opportunities denied his and earlier generations in colonial times, and vowed that his government would do all it could to right past wrongs. Many of his audience, which included academics bearing fraternal greetings from universities all over the world, were embarrassed: some because he cried, others because he did have something to cry about. In Zambia at independence there had been just one state secondary school and one technical college: not at all a proud record of colonial educational achievement.

Education is not a panacea for all the ills of Africa. Indeed it can be argued that there has been an over-reaction to the lost opportunities of colonial times, and many in Africa have caught what has been called the 'diploma disease'. Emphasis has been placed on academic rather than technical subjects and on acquiring qualifications which may be unrelated to jobs available. Employers, including governments, have entered into the spirit of the thing with gusto, making inappropriate qualification demands of job candidates. The system raises expectations which cannot be fulfilled, is geared to urban aspirations and so contributes to problems of accelerating urbanization and serious qualitative rural depopulation.

But at the root of the educational problem literacy itself ought to be a fundamental human right. Not because it is a job qualification but because of its intrinsic value, its basic contribution to the quality of human life. In ten African countries in 1979 less than 10 per cent of the population was literate. They included the four poor, Muslim, land-locked states of the Sahel and poor, Muslim, equally arid Somalia, all states where, among other factors, nomadic life contributed to educational problems. Ethiopia, Angola and Somalia were ravaged by war and excess poverty. Guinea, Senegal and Liberia were less readily explicable except that in Liberia the Americanized élite did not see the need to extend education to the masses. Perhaps Master-Sergeant Doe sees otherwise, perhaps that is why he is now President of Liberia. The literacy problem in Africa is almost universal. Only ten territories have literacy rates above 50 per cent. Tanzania and Zimbabwe alone have literacy rates above 70 per cent. These statistics correlate well with statistics of newspaper circulation, so revealing interesting traditions arising from and themselves encouraging literacy.

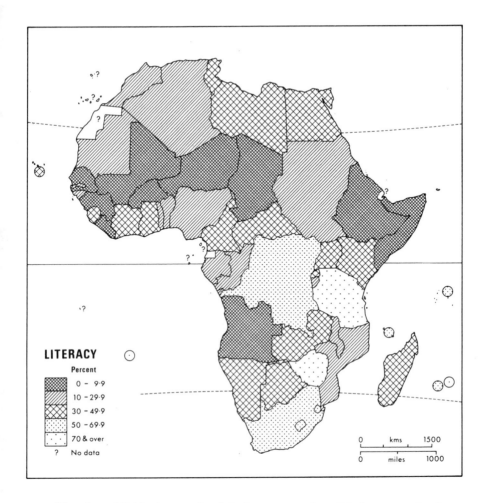

LITERACY

Percent

	0 – 9·9
	10 – 29·9
	30 – 49·9
	50 – 69·9
	70 & over
?	No data

0   kms   1500

0   miles   1000

Uganda and Ethiopia committed the least proportion of their gross national product (GNP) to education at 1.5 per cent and 2 per cent respectively. In contrast thirteen African states spent more than 5 per cent of GNP on education in 1979. Political upheaval and civil war are clearly not conducive to investment in education. But African states are not alone in giving lower priority to education than to guns.

Education in Africa is a problem not only in overall resource terms but also in terms of making education relevant to the needs of the people. Literacy must be conquered because only then can one think of turning out people with the practical skills necessary for running railways and mines, operating factories and above all improving agriculture.

B Historical

11 Africa: cradle of mankind

Archaeologists working in Africa are literally unearthing and piecing together a significant refinement of the theory of human evolution. With due allowance for the ongoing nature of the research, the almost daily discovery of new material, and disputes about precise dating and interpretations, there is emerging from Africa an exciting advance in our understanding of human evolution.

Charles Darwin pointed to Africa as the place most likely to produce evidence for a fuller understanding of 'the descent of man'. That evidence was needed to close the gap in time between the widely known *Ramapithecus* of about 12 million years ago and the equally well-dispersed direct ancestor of man, *Homo erectus*, of 1 million years ago. It was the search for the 'missing link'. In 1924 in a limestone quarry at Taung in the northern Cape Province of South Africa a hominid skull of great significance was found. It was identified and named by Raymond Dart as *Australopithecus africanus*, a biped ape-man. Although reported in the scientific press the discovery was largely ignored. Then in the late 1930s in the Transvaal, other skulls also identified as *Australopithecenes* were found in two forms, *A. africanus* at Sterkfontein and Makapansgat and the large, more thickset *A. robustus* at Kromdraai and Swartkrans. Unfortunately as cave sites they were difficult to date, but apparently, here in Africa was Darwin's missing link. The hypothesis now emerging is more complex.

From 1959 an enormous number of hominid fossil remains have been unearthed in the Rift Valley of east Africa. They have included several examples of *A. africanus* and *A. boisei*, the east-African form of *A. robustus*, dated between 3 and 1.5 million years ago, but also examples of early *Homo* species dating back to 2 million years ago. The existence of two types of *Australopithecus* had already led to a suggestion that the *robustus/boisei* form might be a side-shoot on the evolutionary tree. What Richard Leakey and others have shown is that a form of *Homo* lived contemporaneously with *Australopithecenes*. Their hypothesis is that about 5 million years ago *Ramapithecus* divided into the two *Australopithecene* forms, which later became extinct, and the *Homo* branch of *Homo habilis*, *Homo erectus*, *Homo sapiens* and modern man, *Homo sapiens sapiens*. Some dating doubts remain and further evidence needs to be examined before the hypothesis is universally accepted.

It poses a fascinating geographical conundrum. Why, when *Ramapithecus* and *Homo erectus* are found in Africa, Asia and Europe, is *Australopithecus* found only in Africa south of the Sahara? Are such remains merely awaiting discovery

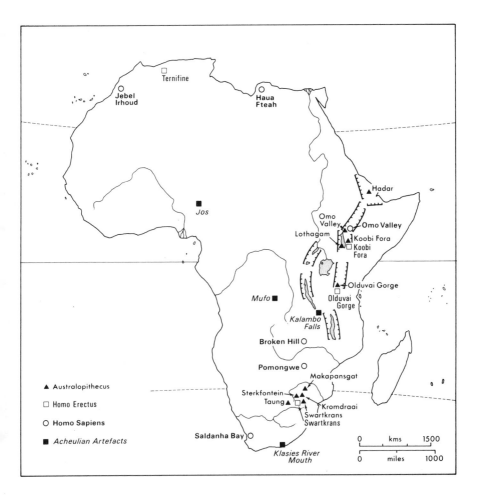

Map legend:

▲ Australopithecus
□ Homo Erectus
○ Homo Sapiens
■ Acheulian Artefacts

Map labels: Ternifine, Jebel Irhoud, Haua Fteah, Hadar, Jos, Omo Valley, Omo Valley, Lothagam, Koobi Fora, Koobi Fora, Olduvai Gorge, Olduvai Gorge, Mufo, Kalambo Falls, Broken Hill, Pomongwe, Makapansgat, Sterkfontein, Taung, Kromdraai, Swartkrans, Swartkrans, Saldanha Bay, Klasies River Mouth

kms 1500
miles 1000

elsewhere, perhaps even in a Sussex gravel pit, or was it that man was somehow confined to Africa in this period of evolution?

Homo erectus sites have been discovered throughout Africa including several sites in the Maghreb, notably Ternifine. *Homo sapiens* sites are also very widely distributed in Africa from Saldanha Bay to Haua Fteah.

Another clue to human pre-history are the tools or artefacts used by early man. Study of Acheulian artefact sites shows that they were widespread in Africa and that use of these tools spread from Africa to Asia and Europe where they represent the first major tool-making tradition. Is this not further evidence pointing to Africa as 'the cradle of mankind'?

12 Pre-European history

As Africa was a cradle of mankind so Egypt was a cradle of civilization. By using simple agricultural techniques, primitive metal tools and the annual flood-waters of the Nile, the Egyptians created one of the earliest, richest and most durable civilizations. Flood irrigation was the key to the Egyptians' ability to produce a regular surplus of food. Their society grew in complexity and their civilization flourished for thousands of years, from before 3000 BC to the Assyrian conquest of 665 BC. The achievements of early Egypt are remarkable, for example in writing, medicine and architecture with all the skills of arts, mathematics, science and engineering implied. The geographical core of Egypt was the Nile delta and lower valley to the first cataract at Aswan. At its greatest extent the Egyptian empire extended southwards to include Nubia and northwards to Syria.

The Assyrians were the first of a succession of Eurasian empires to conquer Egypt and other parts of north Africa. The Persians led by Cambyses came in 525 BC to conquer Egypt and Cyrenaica. Under Darius they completed the first Suez canal, from the Gulf of Suez to the Nile, and established a regular sea-trading route from Egypt to Persia via the Erythraean (Red) Sea.

A little earlier the Phoenician circumnavigation of Africa recorded by Herodotus took place. The Phoenicians were fabled seamen and sea-traders who sailed throughout the Mediterranean, exploited silver mines in Spain, established trading settlements on the Atlantic coastlines west of Gibraltar and founded an empire based on Carthage which eventually became independent.

The Greeks also set up trading settlements on the north African coast as at Cyrene. Alexander the Great visited Egypt to found Alexandria (332 BC) as a new capital for this province of his empire at the western end of the Nile delta coast. It stands as one of the first examples of the colonial port-capital, so familiar to modern Africa. On Alexander's death Egypt became the centre of the kingdom of Ptolemy, one of Alexander's generals. Greek settlements were established as far down the Erythraean coast as Adulis.

The Roman empire was the first to include the whole of the north African coast from Morocco to Egypt and inland as far as the desert. The Romans first had to overcome Carthage led by Hannibal who was defeated at Zama south of Carthage in 202 BC. In 30 BC they finally took Egypt. Rome held sway over north Africa for about 400 years until Rome itself fell. Even then Egypt remained part of the east Roman empire ruled from Constantinople. It was a Christian empire

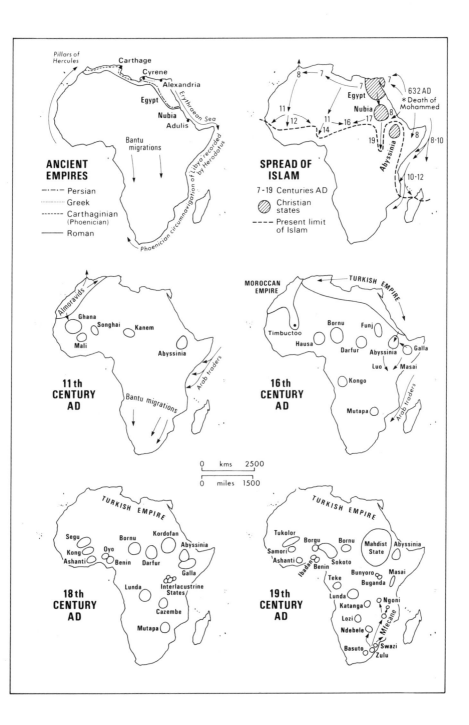

whose missionaries not only made Egypt into a Christian kingdom but also converted Nubia.

Within ten years of the death of the Prophet Mohammed in Medina the Christian kingdom of Egypt had fallen to the Arab Caliphate inspired by the new religion of Islam. By AD 705 the Arabs had conquered as far west as Morocco. Also in the eighth century Islam entered the Horn of Africa and began to spread along the sea-trade route down the east African coast. The Nubian Christian kingdom in the Nile valley and Christian Abyssinia delayed the westward spread of Islam. The Sahara was no such barrier and by the eleventh century Islam had crossed the desert via trade routes to the main Sudanic trading centres. It then spread east and west along the Sahelian corridor between desert and forest. Nubia and the upper Nile valley was overwhelmed very much later to complete the spread of Islam in Africa to its present limits.

Meanwhile in Africa south of the Sahara large-scale, long-distance migrations of peoples were taking place. The Bantu-speaking peoples moved eastwards and southwards from west Africa. By the eleventh century they had reached southern Africa where they came into contact with the San (Bushmen) and Khoi-Khoi (Hottentots) who were gradually pressed into the south-western corner of the continent.

Along the Sahelian corridor several African states arose. Among the earliest in the west were Ghana and Mali, names taken by the modern states, with some geographical licence to acknowledge their political and cultural roots extending back at least 1000 years. In the eleventh century the western Sahelian states were overwhelmed by the Almoravids a puritanical Islamic sect based in Mauritania who vigorously pursued their cause throughout north-western Africa. At the southern end of well-established trans-Saharan trade routes the Sahelian states often had to endure such incursions from the north: it was a locational risk. Trade flourished in gold, salt, ivory and slaves while the grasslands of the Sahel and the fertile area of the Niger inland delta were well able to support the urban populations of the trading centres.

The establishment of European sea-trading posts along the west African coast from the late fifteenth century caused a major decline of the Sahelian trading towns. As products of the west African hinterland were attracted to the coast by the higher prices offered by Europeans so the Sahelian towns found themselves on the periphery of trade not at the centre of it as they had been. As time has passed the effect of that peripheral location has become more marked and the prosperity of the trading towns has dwindled.

In 1591 the Songhai empire was defeated by an army from Morocco which had crossed the Sahara. The western part of the Sahel became a Moroccan colony and although the link with Morocco became more tenuous over the centuries the Moroccan hegemony of that time forms the basis of modern Moroccan claims to the western Sahara, Mauritania and parts of Algeria.

The Sahelian belt spawned many new states, Hausa-land and Bornu are but two examples. Further east Abyssinia survived as a beleaguered island of Christianity in an Islamic sea. In north Africa the Turkish empire extended from Morocco in the west to Eritrea in the south-east. Various Nilotic groups migrated southwards into east Africa. The Bantu state of Kongo emerged as a powerful force in northern Angola. In the south the Mutapa of Great Zimbabwe fame not only built wonderful and mysterious stone structures but also worked copper and gold to sell with ivory to Arab traders who pushed south along the Swahili coast.

In the eighteenth and nineteenth centuries small but significant states emerged in the forest fringe area of west Africa: the Ashanti, Oyo, Ibadan and Benin are important examples. They were rich, their people lived in towns, developed craft industries including metal-working which today form part of the cultural heritage. Ashanti gold-weights and Benin bronzes are magnificent examples of such traditions. In the Sahel the power of individual states waxed and waned. Between the great lakes of east Africa the Bantu kingdoms of Buganda, Bunyoro, Busoga, Ankole, and Toro arose to fight among themselves for supremacy. On the watersheds of central Africa the Lunda, Katanga and Cazembe gained prominence.

In southern Africa in the early nineteenth century population pressure on the land helped cause the emergence of several nations, including the Zulu, Swazi, Basuto and Ndebele, and a tumult of mass migrations known as the *mfecane*. At the centre was the Zulu kingdom built up in a remarkably short period by Shaka. Rewarded for his service to Dingiswayo the paramount chief with the chieftainship of his own small clan, the Zulu, in 1816, Shaka fashioned them into a formidable fighting force. He soon succeeded to the paramountcy and by 1820, through conquest and absorption had made the Zulu the foremost military force in southern Africa. The *mfecane* spread in a series of shock waves from Zululand. Mzilikazi, one of Shaka's *indunas*, formed the Ndebele nation as he fled Shaka's wrath. On the high veld the Ndebele encountered the trek-boers and so migrated north to present-day Zimbabwe to settle around Bulawayo, named after the Zulu royal kraal. Joshua Nkomo is Mzilikazi's political heir and Gatsha Buthelezi is Shaka's.

The pre-European history of Africa is long, complex and fascinating. It owes much to oral traditions which at last are being converted into written records. The African past does exist and a proper understanding of it is very often the key to current political issues in various parts of the continent.

13 European penetration to 1880

In August 1415 Europe's first toe-hold on the African continent was established when the Portuguese captured the port of Ceuta which stands on the north Moroccan coast opposite Gibraltar. Passing to Spain with the union of the Portuguese and Spanish crowns in 1640, Ceuta has remained Spanish to the present day to be, along with Melilla (first occupied by Spain in 1497), Europe's last toe-hold on the African continent.

The occupation of Ceuta was the prelude to the Portuguese voyages of discovery which were to open up the Cape sea route to India. The Portuguese were motivated by a complex mix of Christian zeal against the infidel Muslims, the lure of Guinea gold, the hope of a strategic Christian link-up with the legendary Prester John, and the ultimate prize of the India trade. Encouraged by Prince Henry the Navigator they swept down the west coast of Africa, Cape Bojador (1434), Cape Blanco (1441), Cape Verde (1444) to reach black Africa. By Henry's death in 1460 gold and slaves were established trades and the west African coast was known as far as Sierra Leone. By 1482 the Portuguese had fortified trading posts on the coast from Senegambia to the Gold Coast and had succeeded in diverting much of the ancient trans-Saharan trade. Diego Cao 'discovered' the mouth of the River Zaire (Congo) in 1484 and two years later reached Cape Cross. Bartholomeu Dias soon followed to round the Cape of Good Hope and plant his furthest *padrao* at Kwaaihoek in March 1488. There was then a mysterious nine-year delay before Vasco da Gama rounded the Cape, paused briefly at Mossel Bay before sailing past Natal on Christmas Day 1497, to arrive at Malindi in April 1498. There picking up a pilot, Da Gama had a quick passage to India on the summer monsoon, arriving at Calicut on 20 May 1498.

On the east African coast the Portuguese captured a string of Swahili trading ports from Sofala and Quelimane in the south to Mombasa, Malindi and Lamu in the north. The main trade of the east coast was gold and ivory but in rather disappointing quantities, discouraging penetration of the interior except along the lower Zambezi valley. In the north-east the Portuguese did establish contact with their Prester John, leader of Christian Ethiopia, but he was far less powerful than had been hoped and rather than being able to join them in a new crusade was himself sorely threatened by Islam on all sides.

On the west coast Portuguese trade flourished in gold, silver, ivory, hides and, above all, slaves. From their coastal trading posts two great slave entrepôts of Sao Tomé and Santiago the Portuguese shipped slaves to their plantations in Brazil and to Spanish America. Later Luanda (1575) and Benguela (1617) also became

36

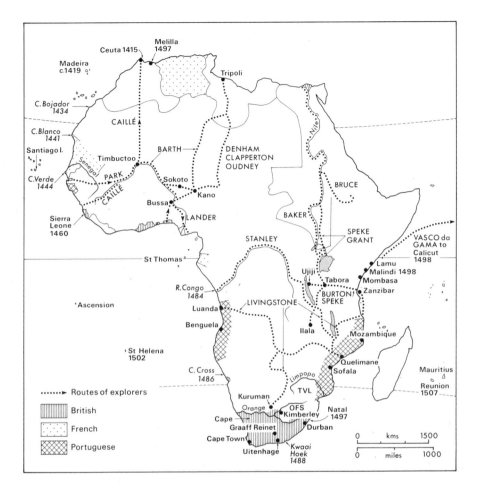

Routes of explorers

British

French

Portuguese

prominent in the slave trade, and from these the Portuguese penetrated the hinterland of Angola.

In the seventeenth century Portuguese supremacy on the route to India was challenged as East India companies were formed by the British (1600), Dutch (1602), French (1604) and Danes (1610). The Dutch actually held Luanda and Benguela between 1641 and 1648 before establishing their own victualling station at Cape Town in 1652. The British set up a station at St Helena (1659) after the Dutch, the French at Ile de Bourbon (Reunion) in 1642 and in 1715, also in succession to the Dutch, at Ile de France (Mauritius).

All the European maritime nations established posts on the west African coast to trade in slaves, gold and ivory. But European interest in Africa was limited to these coastal trading posts and victualling stations. Up-country trading was generally conducted by proxy. There was little penetration of the interior except by the French along the Senegal river and by the Dutch from the Cape.

Within five years of the Dutch East India Company setting up its station free burghers were settled at the Cape. By the end of the eighteenth century Dutch farmers (Boers) had spread slowly eastwards into the unpromising interior, practising extensive cattle-ranching in a semi-arid environment to establish small settlements at Graaff Reinet (1786) and Uitenhage (1804). To keep it out of French hands in the Napoleonic wars the British took the Cape from the Dutch (1795), returned it to the Batavian Republic (1803) and finally reoccupied it in 1806. In 1814 Britain kept the Cape, paying the Dutch an indemnity of £6 million. It was a fateful decision which led to the opening-up of the interior by the Dutch Boers. Disgruntled with British justice at Slaghters Nek, British incompetence in dealing with the frontier situation, and British trickery in paying compensation for the abolition of slavery in distant London, the Boers decided to trek into the interior away from the Cape Colony. They crossed the Orange river eventually to found the Orange Free State. Some went on across the Vaal and later formed the South African Republic (Transvaal), while others went down into Natal to found the Republic of Natalia. Within months the European frontier in southern Africa was extended inland a thousand miles, if a little precariously. Many Africans were displaced in long-drawn-out conflict which involved the strongest groups, the Zulu, Ndebele and Basuto. The British took the comparatively easy sea route to Durban, claimed Natal for their own and pushed the Boers out. When diamonds were found on Boer farms east of the Vaal river in 1870 the land quickly came under British 'protection': capitalism and imperialism were beginning to walk hand in hand.

The London Missionary Society had preceded the trek-boers over the Orange river to found their most famous mission at Kuruman (1816) from which the next stage of European penetration of southern Africa began in 1841 in the person of David Livingstone. First to Lake Ngami, then to the Zambezi at Sesheke and on to Luanda on the west coast Livingstone tramped: he retraced his footsteps to Sesheke, then down the Zambezi to behold 'Scenes such as angels must have gazed upon in their flights', and name the Victoria Falls. He continued down the great river to Quelimane on the east coast where the inevitable British brig soon came to return him to London via Mauritius and the Red Sea. Livingstone was the first European to cross Africa, but was not the first major European, or even Scots, explorer of Africa.

James Bruce had followed the Blue Nile into the highlands of Ethiopia in 1766 and in the west yet another Scot, Mungo Park, had reached the upper Niger in 1796 and returned to sail down that river to his death at Bussa in 1806. Denham, Clapperton and Oudney crossed the Sahara from Tripoli to Kano and Sokoto;

Clapperton with Lander returned to Kano via the west African coast only to die there; Lander with his brother sailed down the Niger from Bussa to its mouth: all that in the period 1823–30. In 1827 René Caillé set out, in disguise, for the fabled golden city of Timbuctoo but the reality he reported was so dull and earthy that few believed he had even been there. Barth, the German emissary of the Royal Geographical Society, finally laid the legend of Timbuctoo in a five-year expedition reported in five stout volumes.

Meanwhile the quest for the source of the Nile was underway. Burton and Speke from Zanzibar to Lake Tanganyika, Speke to Lake Victoria, Speke and Grant down the Nile, to breakfast with Sam Baker and his lady on their grand way to Lake Albert, and then home to dispute with Burton and the arm-chair geographers. Livingstone returned to the Zambezi but it was not 'God's highway to the heart of Africa', so he turned northwards to ensure that Malawi would be second home for future Scots missionaries. On his last journey Livingstone continued his crusade against the Arab slave trade and joined in the Nile quest to die, a lonely broken man, at Ilala.

Before he died Livingstone himself had been 'discovered' at Ujiji by Stanley in 1872, with the incredible greeting 'Dr Livingstone I presume'. Stanley, fatherless son of a Welsh workhouse, 'adopted' Livingstone and his theory that the Lualaba was in fact the Nile. He got off to a bad start when the president of the Royal Geographical Society declined even to believe that he had found Livingstone. Stanley survived to become the greatest, if one of the most ruthless, of all the European explorers of Africa. He circumnavigated Lake Victoria and then Lake Tanganyika, crossed to the Lualaba and followed it 2000 miles (3200 km)'through the Dark Continent' to the west coast. Alas, Livingstone had been wrong, but the mystery of the Nile and the Congo had finally been resolved in one epic, brutal journey. Stanley twice returned to Africa on major expeditions both closely associated with the next phase of Europe's affair with Africa – the scramble. The explorers collectively combined missionary zeal with scientific enquiry and were not averse to keeping an eye open for prospects of trade. They excited European interest in Africa with their fascinating tales and wonderful books and paved the way for the impending scramble.

39

14 Slave trades

When the Portuguese reached west Africa in the mid-fifteenth century they were eager to trade. After braving the hostile, barren western Sahara coast they reached a green land (Cape Verde), rich in prized items of trade (Ivory Coast, Gold Coast, SLAVE coast). West African slaves were traded in Portugal as early as 1444 but it was not until the Americas started to be opened up in the sixteenth century that the slave trade really got under way. This infamous trade prospered because in the Americas the plantation system of agriculture created an almost insatiable demand for slaves. The supply of slaves in west Africa presented no major problem so that European traders willing to indulge in the traffic could, and did, make enormous profits.

In its most notorious and highly developed form the slave trade was a 'triangular' trade. Cheap goods from Europe, mainly England, were carried to the west coast of Africa to be traded with African middlemen for slaves who were cargo for the 'middle passage' to the Americas where they were sold. With the proceeds were purchased products of slave labour, sugar, cotton and tobacco, to sell in Europe at great profit. A small reinvestment in a cargo of cheap goods started the cycle all over again. While the English were the most prominent, all European seafaring nations indulged in the slave trade, Danes, Dutch, French, Germans, Portuguese and Spaniards. The Portuguese established slave entrepôts at Sao Tomé and Santiago but their greatest trade was from Angola to Brazil, and Luanda was for a long time the largest slave port on the west African coast. Early in the nineteenth century as many as 135,000 slaves a year were taken across the Atlantic.

The depredations of the slave trade make a catalogue of horror from the basic human indignity to the brutal decimation of whole populations. Village was set against village, tribe against tribe in violent campaigns of terror fought for human booty. Towards the end of the eighteenth century the revulsion of it all began to sink in with more enlightened leaders in England. A long hard struggle fought by men like William Wilberforce gained first the abolition of the slave trade (1807) and then the abolition of slavery itself in the British empire (1833). In the tradition of a thief to catch a thief the ubiquitous British navy kept itself in fighting trim through the middle years of the nineteenth century stamping out the slave trade wherever it could.

That included the Arab slave trade on the east coast of Africa, centred for centuries on Zanzibar. The Arab traders, unlike their European counterparts in the west, penetrated deeply into the hinterland. European explorers encountered

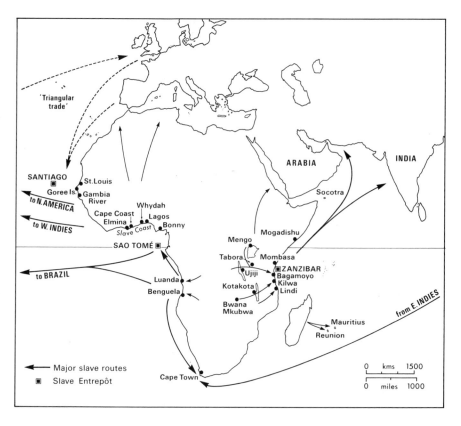

Arab slave parties in Malawi, along the well-defined Bagamoyo to Ujiji trade route, in Uganda and the Sudan and as far west as the Lualaba river where the slave trader Tippu Tib held sway to the discomfiture of Stanley's ill-fated 'rear column' as late as 1888.

The significance of four centuries of widespread slavery is enormous, if only its contribution to European economic development and African underdevelopment, to racial prejudice and multiracial societies. Slavery persisted into this century, in some forms survives today, and the Anti-Slavery Society of London still remains active.

15 The scramble for Africa

There was a marked geographical symmetry to the beginnings of colonization in Africa as European settlers were attracted to the warm temperate climates of Algeria and South Africa. Then in 1869 the historical coincidence of the opening of the Suez canal and the diamond rush in South Africa simultaneously transformed both ends of the continent.

The significance of diamonds to the subsequent history of southern Africa and the scramble is not easily exaggerated. Britain had taken the Cape during the Napoleonic wars to safeguard the route to India. It was inconvenient that the Cape station was part of a colony, and costly and painful that the colony should have an unstable frontier disputed by expansionist Boers and expansionist Xhosas. British imperial attitudes waxed and waned. Money was reluctantly voted, frontier wars waged and territory annexed; but money was also withheld, peace made and land returned. Such changes often reflected changes in government in Westminster and swung with the fortunes of Tories and Liberals. The most dramatic swing came in 1881 when, after a period of expansion which included the annexation of the Transvaal and the Zulu war, the newly elected Gladstone government made peace following the British defeat at Majuba, granting the Transvaal its independence, but retaining undefined British 'suzerainty'. The net result of the swing of the imperial pendulum in South Africa was, however, of British territorial expansion on the basis of two steps forward, one step back.

Kimberley added a new dimension to British imperialism in Africa, a financial rationale for territorial expansion which united local settler interests with metropolitan capitalists. It facilitated the subsequent exploitation of the Witwatersrand gold-fields and through Lenin's adaptation of Hobson's polemic gave rise to the thesis of 'imperialism the highest stage of capitalism'. The botched Jameson Raid of 1895 and the Anglo-Boer war of 1899–1902 were classical manifestations of capitalist imperialism. The irony is that the immediate victims were the Boers who had been cheated out of the diamond-fields by boundary 'adjustment', then steam-rollered by a vast imperial army dedicated to the cause of capitalism cloaked by appalling jingoism. The Boers had already carved their settler republics out of conquered lands and they were now quick to learn from the British.

The Suez canal was the key to the Middle East route to India. A personal triumph for Ferdinand de Lesseps, the canal was engineered in the face of determined opposition from Britain who feared the long-term strategic

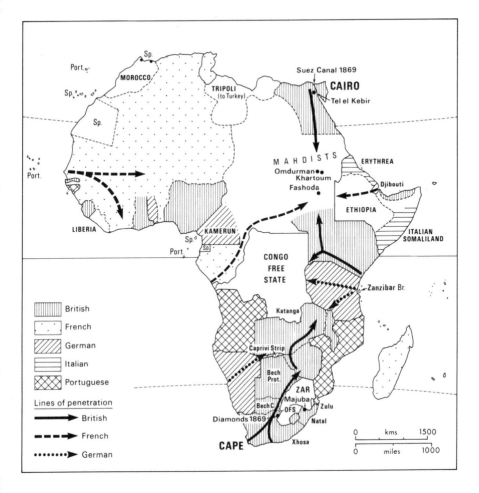

consequences of French control. Disraeli's swift move of 1875 to buy the
Khedive's shares in the Canal Company for £4 million was, in fact, welcomed by
de Lesseps and in 1876 Britain and France assumed joint control of Egypt's
financial affairs. In 1882 the canal was threatened by the Arabi revolt and Britain
intervened to safeguard her investment, won the battle of Tel-el-Kebir and
occupied Egypt. France having declined to join in military intervention 'faded
politically from the Egyptian scene'.

Egypt had conquered the Sudan in 1820–1 and had built up a regionally based
administration which, in later years, employed British and other European
officers. In 1881 the revolt of the Mahdi began and spread throughout the Sudan
leading to the expulsion of the Egyptians and the death of Gordon at Khartoum

43

in 1885. Emin Pasha, Governor of Equatoria Province, became a refugee from the Mahdi's forces to be unwillingly rescued by the intrepid Stanley in 1889 on his last major expedition 'in darkest Africa'.

Britain, now in occupation of Egypt, eventually determined to push up the Nile. Security of the route to India, for 300 years a main plank of British foreign policy, now required control of Suez, which in crisis required the occupation of Egypt, which in turn was secure only when the Sudan was safe, given that Uganda, at the source of the Nile, was already 'protected' (1894).

The final act of dispute between the European powers on the Nile was near comic opera. In 1896 the French sent a small party under Major Marchand on an epic transcontinental journey from the Congo to the Nile, there to meet with a second French force moving west from Djibouti with Ethiopian support. Against all odds Marchand reached Fashoda in 1898 to await the Djibouti force. It failed to arrive, having been decimated by disease and sickness on descending into the hot plains from the Ethiopian highlands. Instead, up the Nile, fresh from his triumph at Omdurman (September 1898), came Kitchener at the head of a large Anglo-Egyptian army. The French force of 8 officers, 3 NCOs and 130 Sengalese troops stood its ground to act out the diplomatic charade of the 'Fashoda incident'. Eventually the French withdrew with honour, leaving the British in control of the Nile from Uganda to the sea, a position confirmed by the French in the 1904 *entente* in return for 'a free hand in Morocco'.

Rivalry between the European powers for reasons of trade, strategic advantage or simply prestige was at the heart of the scramble for Africa. Bismarck's extension of German imperial protection to the trader Luderitz in South West Africa in 1883 precipitated a flurry of British activity, imperial and local South African. The perceived danger was of Germany from the west linking with the Boer republics to cut 'the road to the north'. In quick succession the western boundary of the Transvaal was fixed, the two tiny Boer republics of Stellaland and Goshen were eliminated, Bechuanaland Protectorate proclaimed and British Bechuanaland annexed.

The discovery of the immensely rich Witwatersrand gold-fields in 1886 further whetted British appetites for the drive into the interior. In 1890 Rhodes, armed with a Royal Charter and dubious 'concessions', launched his pioneer column to Mashonaland. The Ndebele were conquered in 1893 and again in 1896 with the aid of the Maxim gun. Amid cries of 'Cape to Cairo' the railway reached Bulawayo in late 1897 and British South Africa Company rule was established on both banks of the Zambezi.

Meanwhile in 1884–5 the European powers met in Berlin to construct the rules for the 'great game of scramble'. They declared a free trade zone across central Africa encompassing entirely the Congo Free State which became in effect the private colony of Leopold, King of the Belgians, through his International

Association. 'The General Act of the Conference of Berlin' recognized European 'spheres of influence' in Africa and provided such rules as 'occupations on the coast of Africa in order to be valid must be effective, and any new occupation on the coast must be formally notified to the Signatory Powers'.

The particular motives for declaring a sphere of influence varied as Europeans, convinced of their 'civilizing role', the 'truth' of their religion and their right to trade, strove to exploit Africa and to compete with each other, for the most part harmlessly for themselves, but not for Africa. For the Europeans it *did* become a gigantic game, some super 'Monopoly', played with real land and real people. Zanzibar was traded for Heligoland, Cameroun became Kamerun for 'a free hand in Morocco'.

Almost all the European nations had established trading posts along the west African coast. By the mid-nineteenth century many had ceased trading and some rationalization of European interests was achieved with the British and French most influential, but they failed to agree to a proposed grand division between themselves. Penetration from the coast was a slow process and came with sharp punitive expeditions such as that led by Wolseley against the King of Ashanti at Kumasi in 1873. When spheres of influence were established under the rules of the scramble they were extended inland from short stretches of coast giving rise to a pattern of long narrow colonies. The French advanced inland from Dakar on the Senegal–Niger route and were thus able not only to forestall British penetration of the far interior but also to link up with their own colonies in Ivory Coast and Dahomey. West Africa thus became the most fragmented part of the African coastline with twelve different colonial territories between Cape Blanco and Calabar.

So Africa was divided up and provided with its sometimes strange colonial boundaries. The Germans insisted on having access to the Zambezi and so the finger of the Caprivi strip was drawn on Europe's map of Africa, although access to the Zambezi through that strip was not a practical proposition. The Katanga pedicle, defined by a watershed which when they went to look could hardly be found on the ground, fortuitously divided the central African copperbelt. When in doubt the straight line was employed, lines of latitude and longitude and failing them any old straight line even with kinks around mountains, as with Kilimanjaro which apparently was not Queen Victoria's birthday present to her grandson the Kaiser Wilhelm II.

The scramble was a division of Africa by Europeans for Europeans. There was scant regard to Africa let alone to Africans. Its geographical importance lies in the fact that the colonial boundaries became, with little change, the territorial framework for African independence.

16 Colonial Africa

By 1914 the political map of colonial Africa was complete and there was little subsequent change. Within fifty years the colonial boundary mesh would become the almost exact basis for territorial division of independent Africa then to be made immutable by resolution of the Organization of African Unity (OAU) in 1964.

In 1910 the four British colonies in South Africa were united as the Union of South Africa almost as a compensatory gesture for the Anglo-Boer war which many British Liberals had bitterly opposed. Voices were raised to urge extension of the multiracial Cape franchise to all parts of the new Union but they were silenced by the expediency of seeing the settlement through. Few envisaged separate voters' rolls and the disenfranchisement of non-whites in the Cape. The three southern African protectorates were, for the time being, excluded from the Union. Company rule ended in Southern Rhodesia in 1923 and whites there opted for 'responsible self-government' rather than join the Union for which provision had been made. Britain took another critical decision in 1914 to rule Nigeria as a single colony. Although in 1939 the territory was divided into three regions, Nigeria remained united.

The First World War spilled over into Africa. British, French, Belgian and South African forces variously defeated German colonial armies except that of Von Lettow Vorbeck, who emerged from the east African bush at the end of 1918 as the only undefeated German general, to be feted as such on his return to Berlin. The Allied powers shared their German spoils. Togo and Kamerun were both divided between France and Britain. France got the larger share of each and ruled them as separate territories. Britain administered her acquisitions as part of the Gold Coast (Ghana) and Nigeria respectively. German East Africa (Tanganyika) became British except for Ruanda-Urundi which, being contiguous with the now *Belgian* Congo, went to 'gallant little Belgium'. To reward Italy Britain ceded Jubaland from Kenya to Italian Somaliland. German South West Africa (Namibia) having been conquered by Botha and Smuts in 1915 was given to South Africa whose fitness for the task was not doubted. Germany's former African colonies became League of Nations mandates to be administered by the Allies in 'sacred trust'. In 1945 the 'trust' was transferred from the League of Nations to the United Nations, a transfer later disputed by South Africa over Namibia. Trust status was to play a significant role in the decolonization process.

Britain gave up control of the affairs of Egypt in 1922. Fuad became king, to be succeeded by his son Farouk in 1936. Britain, however, retained military control

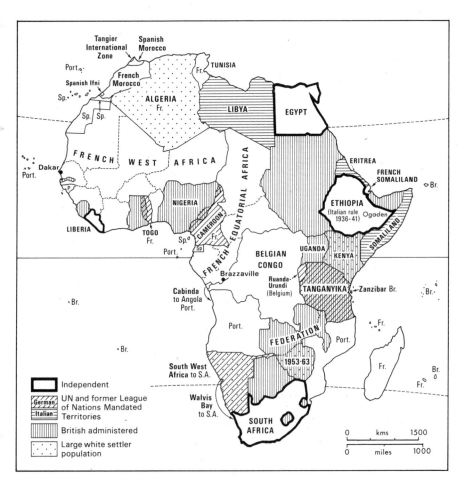

of the Suez canal by means of a large garrison stationed within a newly defined Canal Zone. Ethiopia had successfully resisted an Italian attempt at military conquest by winning the battle of Adowa in 1896, although by the rules of the scramble Ethiopia was regarded by the European powers as an Italian sphere of influence. When Mussolini came to power he determined to reassert Italy's claim to Ethiopia. Britain and France agreed to stand aside in the infamous, secret Hoare–Laval pact, and in October 1935 the Italian army was launched on Ethiopia. Gallant defence was to no avail, the Emperor Haile Selassie fled to Geneva to try to stir the conscience of the League of Nations but at that time (30 June 1936) it had none.

In the Second World War Africa again became a battleground for warring

47

European powers and again colonies changed hands. Italian forces isolated in Somalia, Eritrea and Ethiopia were easily overcome for Haile Selassie to re-enter his capital five years to the day after the Italians had marched in, 5 May 1941. By early 1943 the Germans and Italians had been driven from north Africa. Britain assumed administrative control over Eritrea, Somalia, the Ogaden region of Ethiopia and the two Libyan provinces of Cyrenaica and Tripolitania. France administered the Fezzan province of Libya. Ethiopia's independence was recognized but British proposals for a Greater Somalia were rejected by the United States and the Soviet Union so Somaliland was returned to Italian administration in 1950 and the Ogaden to Ethiopia in 1955.

When the United Nations was formed in 1945 there were just four African member states: Egypt, Ethiopia, Liberia and South Africa. There were five former League of Nations' mandated territories and three other UN trust territories. Portugal held three mainland and two island colonies; Spain two mainland colonies and several enclaves in Morocco; Belgium the Congo and Ruanda-Urundi. The remainder comprised the two vast colonial empires of Britain and France.

From early this century France ruled her African mainland possessions in two large federal blocks, *Afrique Occidentale Française* (AOF) 1902, and *Afrique Equatoriale Française* (AEF) 1908. Administered by governors-general at Dakar and Brazzaville respectively, they returned elected representatives to the French National Assembly in Paris. Although they excluded the UN trust territories of Togo and Cameroon the federations were enormous, AOF with eight territories covered 1.8 million square miles (4.7 million sq. km), AEF with four territories of 1 million square miles (2.5 million sq. km), both larger than Africa's largest independent state of today. The UN trust territories of Togo and Cameroon set the pace in political development but by the mid-1950s most of French Africa seemed very far away from independence. Then a rush of events resulted in the multiple birth of, not twins, but fourteen new states on the African mainland, plus Madagascar. As so often happens with multiple births several of the progeny were weak and needful of postnatal attention which France was eager to provide with intensive neo-colonial care.

Britain also experimented with federation, albeit of a very different kind, when in 1953 the Federation of Rhodesia and Nyasaland was formed. Federation was strongly opposed, within the territories and in Britain itself, by many who saw it as a device for extending white settler rule. Hailed by its supporters as the new millennium the federation lasted a mere decade, a long time in African politics, and not the last occasion politicians were to get their estimates of time wildly wrong in this part of Africa. The federation was seen as a bold new Elizabethan venture in racial partnership. It was contrasted with the negative apartheid state of South Africa which the Afrikaner National Party had been grimly building since 1948. Enthusiasts pointed to the economic complementarity of the territories. The harnessing of the Zambezi at Kariba (1960) linking north and south encapsulated the spirit of co-operation. The new (1955) direct railway line to Lourenço Marques (Maputo) symbolized independence from South Africa. The critics were proved right more quickly than most had anticipated. The reality of discrimination mocked the concept of racial partnership. Black political aspirations were not realized. Northern mineral resources were systematically 'ripped-off' to help finance southern development. Federal allocation decisions almost inevitably favoured the south. Arguments could always be found to support such decisions: better infrastructure, larger local market, more suitable labour, but the cumulative effect was intolerable. Federation finally foundered on African nationalism led by men who had never accepted it and saw no benefits accruing to their people or their territories. In retrospect it seems strange that Dr Banda was the key figure in the break-up of the federation which was the immediate prelude of independence for Malawi and Zambia.

In Southern Rhodesia colonialism, if by another name, was to continue for more than fifteen years. In all African countries with large settler populations the pattern was similar: delayed independence and violence. The French *colons* of Algeria fought to prevent independence only to be sold out by the autocrat they trusted and had helped to bring to power in France, General de Gaulle. In Kenya Mau Mau and settler resistance delayed independence until the end of 1963, two years after Tanganyika and more than a year after Uganda. This delay did not improve the prospects of the East African Community. Many common services had been developed between Kenya, Uganda and Tanganyika under British rule. Shared facilities built up over a long period included posts and telegraphs, customs and excise, railways and harbours, currency, university and an airline. The final steps of welding the territories together into a single political unit was never seriously contemplated by the British who were eventually content to hand over a partially completed task to three newly independent states.

Britain and France, in the administration of their African territories, clearly saw a need to create larger economic units. Yet they gave independence to the individual constituent parts of their federations knowing that once institutionalized even the least viable of states is most unlikely to surrender its sovereignty willingly. Was it a case of deliberate 'divide and rule' as many have subsequently accused? If it was, there were many willing African accomplices each aspiring to leadership of his own small territory. On the other hand where a federation did survive, in Nigeria, a bloody civil war had to be fought to maintain federal unity within a decade of independence.

17 Advance of independence

Zimbabwe became the fifty-first African state in 1980 and so, in one generation, forty-seven new states had been born to give Africa more seats at the UN than any other continent, but still not enough political clout to ensure the election of an African secretary-general in 1981.

The climate conducive to decolonization in Africa evolved outside Africa. Its elements included the Second World War, the Atlantic Charter, the UN, the exhaustion of Europe, the independence of India and the emergence of superpowers dedicated to ending at least overt colonialism.

The UN trust territories led the way in their respective parts of Africa. The administrative powers were accountable to the UN, but more importantly there was explicit expectation of, and set timetables for, independence. Within the African empires of Britain, France and Belgium what was appropriate for trust territories could hardly be inappropriate for other colonies. By splendid irony the territorial booty of two world wars became the Achilles heel of European imperialism in Africa. The Iberian empires in Africa persisted longer, held by insensitive dictatorships until their metropolitan bases crumbled.

The UN set timetables for independence in Libya (1951) and Somalia (1960) but chose for Italy's other African colony, Eritrea, federation with Ethiopia. This led to full union in 1962 and then, almost inevitably, to secessionist war. Eritreans were denied the right of self-determination because American strategic interests favoured a strong Ethiopia with a Red Sea coastline. Russia supported full independence for Eritrea. In 1974 the wheel turned: Russia is now Ethiopia's arms supplier and military adviser in an increasingly bitter war to put down the Eritrean secessionists and, appropriately enough, has a Red Sea naval base.

Egypt's revolution of 1952 hastened the British hand in the Sudan condominium. In Morocco, divided between France and Spain, the independence movement put the French under pressure until, increasingly embroiled in Algeria, they decided to leave. Spain followed suit but even so the five colonial areas of Morocco became independent on five different dates. Spain still retains Melilla and, mockingly opposite Gibraltar, Ceuta. Tunisia also gained independence in 1956 as France further cut her north African commitments to defend the settler colony of Algeria.

Ghana became the first black African state to gain its independence from colonial rule in 1957. The Gold Coast had set the pace and the pattern for political development in British black Africa. Kwame Nkrumah, invited back

50

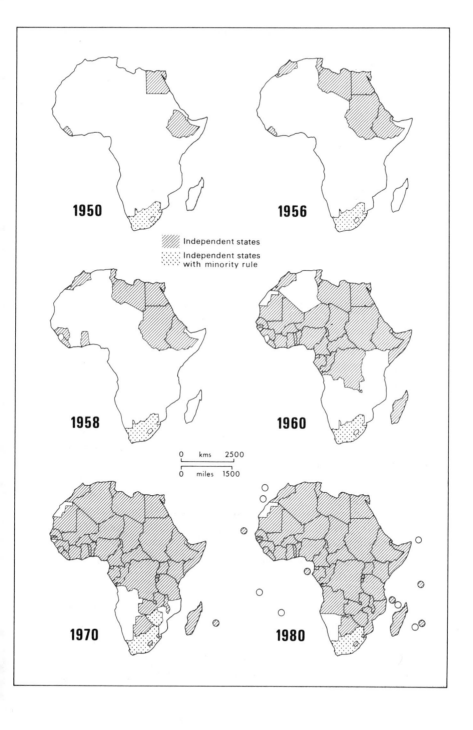

1950

1956

Independent states

Independent states
with minority rule

1958

1960

0   kms   2500
0   miles   1500

1970

1980

from self-imposed exile to the secretaryship of the major independence party in 1947, organized demonstrations, went to jail, was released, formed his own more radical party, organized further campaigns, went to jail again, won the first election from jail, was released to head the first African administration, won further elections before internal self-government, and yet again before independence when he became the first prime minister. This pattern of progress, with minor variations, was to be repeated in colonies throughout British Africa.

French Africa came to independence by a different route. The black colonial élite was assimilated into French culture and society and its political leaders were elected to the National Assembly in Paris. Independence became an issue only after the *Loi Cadre* of 1956 at the initiative of the metropolitan government and applied to all colonies. The federal structures of the AOF and AEF were abandoned in favour of administration based on individual territories. This policy change was strongly supported by Felix Houphouët-Boigny of the Ivory Coast who served in the French cabinet from 1956 to 1959. Others, less conservative, denounced it as balkanization

General de Gaulle, coming to power in 1958, gave each African territory the stark choice of immediate, ill-prepared and unsupported independence or membership of the French Community. Guinea alone voted for independence and forthwith was ruthlessly abandoned. Two years later the other French territories, irrespective of individual preparedness, were moved *en masse* to independence. The year of 1960 saw fourteen French colonies transformed into independent states.

In mid-1960 the Congo (Zaire) became independent to be immediately plunged into an orgy of violence. Belgium had done little to prepare the Congo and at the last moment advanced independence by one year. The few political groups to emerge were organized, divisively, on a regional basis. Within three months of independence the army seized power, arrested prime minister Patrice Lumumba and delivered him to secessionist Katanga (Shaba) where he was murdered in January 1961. The prolonged chaos in the Congo, the atrocities and the human suffering have to be placed at the door of Belgian politicians who, over-anxious to wash their hands of a troublesome responsibility, found themselves washing in blood.

Nigeria also came to independence in 1960 after delay which was resolved by the adoption of a federal constitution which kept the whole colony together as a single state. It was a Nigerian rather than an imposed British solution. Nevertheless the regional differences which had so concerned the pre-independence conferences became the root causes of the civil war of 1967–70. The British empire in Africa continued to be disbanded in a piecemeal but careful fashion, each territory being treated individually according to its preparedness for independence as judged by the British – not always as objectively as claimed. In 1961 Sierra Leone became independent while the UN trust territory of Tanganyika led the way in east Africa.

The turmoil in the Congo (Zaire) was overtaken by the struggle in Algeria which had first erupted in 1954 between nationalists and white *colons*. De Gaulle having come to power with French Algerian support came to see the folly of attempting to hold Algeria by force of arms. He dramatically announced a cease-fire and, following the formality of a referendum, by July 1962 Algeria was independent.

Tribal differences led to separation of Ruanda-Urundi into Rwanda and Burundi in 1962 but could not prevent post-independence massacres on a genocidal scale. In Uganda tribal differences which coincided with progressive/conservative divisions were resolved by a constitution of elaborate checks and balances which was rudely swept aside within four years of independence.

In Kenya, after a decade of sporadic violence, Britain accepted the inevitable and granted independence in 1963 under Jomo Kenyatta. Vilified, jailed, elected, released, elected again, he turned out to be a conservative leader who could even tolerate a white settler in his cabinet.

The Federation of Rhodesia and Nyasaland was broken up and, under Hastings Banda and Kenneth Kaunda respectively, Malawi and Zambia emerged. Britain also decided at this time to bring to independence a number of smaller, weaker territories of doubtful economic and political viability. The Gambia, Botswana, Lesotho, Swaziland and Mauritius all became independent in the period 1966–8. To some extent the British hand was forced because the alternative for the High Commission Territories was union with South Africa, which was nevertheless allowed to extend its economic control over them by the customs agreement of 1970.

Encouraged by British political ineptitude white settler Rhodesia made its unilateral declaration of independence (UDI) in 1965 and for over fourteen years defied all attempts to overturn it. For all the charade of sanctions and British frigates blockading Beira but ignoring Lourenço Marques (Maputo), Rhodesia's undoing was the fall of the Portuguese empire in Africa. Once FRELIMO had achieved power in Mozambique, closed the border to Rhodesian trade and opened their territory to the Patriotic Front, Rhodesia's days were numbered. A new railway link to South Africa and a last minute attempt at power-sharing could not save the minority regime. At the end of 1979 colonial rule was formally re-established and in April 1980 Robert Mugabe emerged as the prime minister of Zimbabwe. As with Kenyatta, and many other Africans before him, Mugabe was soon seen to be not the terrorist monster he had been painted by sections of the British media but a leader anxious to get down to the enormous task of advancing his country and his people.

There remains the problem of the former German colony of South West

Africa, Namibia. South Africa is resisting independence by fighting the South West Africa People's Organization (SWAPO) in the field and by procrastinating at the negotiating table. The western 'contact' group although working for an early settlement largely to safeguard its interests was able to make little progress. Applying its policy of 'constructive engagement' with South Africa the Reagan administration in the United States took over the role of the 'contact' group and connived at South African delaying tactics, and even encouraged them by introducing withdrawal of Cuban troops in Angola as a precondition for implementing the UN timetable for withdrawal from Namibia under Resolution 345. Beyond Namibia is South Africa. Independent since 1910 but on the basis of minority rule it presents a colonial problem with a difference and without doubt the most difficult of all.

C Political

18 States of modern Africa

The states of modern Africa are essentially colonial creations transformed into independent states. Their boundaries, shapes and sizes are part of the colonial inheritance. Mainland Africa has forty-five independent states and three dependent territories, and there are six independent island states and eight dependent island groups. The states come in all shapes and sizes.

According to the rules of the 'great game of scramble' in Africa a European power first had to establish a claim to a stretch of African coastline and was then able to declare as its legitimate sphere of influence territory directly inland. The length of coastline claimed depended on how near on either side of its own trading post was the next post of another European power. On the coveted west African coastline trading posts were strung together like beads on a string. Even after rationalization in the nineteenth century some claims were for very short lengths of coastline.

The former British colony of Gambia was based on a trading post, Bathurst, now Banjul, at the mouth of the Gambia river. The sphere of influence inland was defined in terms of that river which was the main trading artery. The result is a state over 200 miles (320 km) long with a maximum width of 30 miles (48 km). The former German colony, Togo, has a 44 mile (70 km) coastline but extends inland about 340 miles (545 km); its neighbour Benin, the former French colony of Dahomey, has a coastline of 62 miles (100 km) and an inland extent of 410 miles (655 km). While no detailed research has examined the relationship between territorial shape and the economic development process, such extreme shapes must lead to strong regional contrasts which suggest a prima facie case for saying that they do not help development.

The total area of Africa is over 11.5 million square miles (30 million sq. km). Eighty per cent of the area is divided between twenty-one states, 20 per cent between forty-one territories. One of the most pertinent facts of African political geography is that seven independent states are smaller in area than Wales, and *together* make up only one-eighth of 1 per cent of the total area of the continent. While thirty-one African states have an area greater than that of the United Kingdom, only one, Nigeria, has a greater population. Twelve independent African states have a population of under 1 million. St Thomas and Prince Islands, and the Seychelles have populations of less than 150,000. If the Seychelles played Wales at rugby football, their entire population could give support in the Cardiff Arms Park, and still leave room for several thousand Welsh supporters to keep them in tune. If a third criterion of size is used, wealth

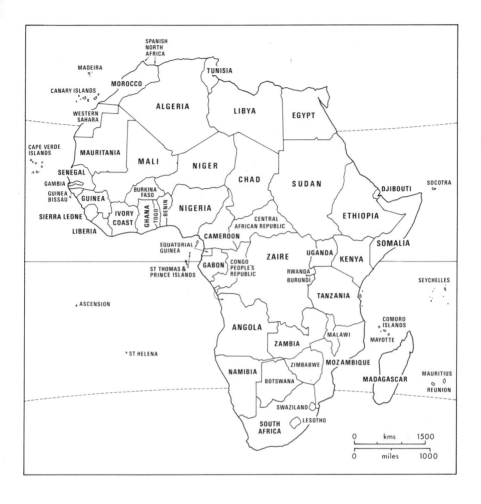

– as measured by gross national product (GNP) – then the contrast between rich and poor within Africa and between the smaller African countries and the rest of the world is even greater. In 1980 sixteen African countries had a GNP of less than US $1 billion and three of US $100 million or less. In 1983 a single British frigate cost over US $150 million. For a variety of reasons, most with roots in the colonial past, many African states are, by a number of criteria, very small. Their extreme smallness brings into question their economic and political viability and renders them vulnerable to forces of neo-colonialism.

19 A political pecking order

Africa is a continent of fifty-one independent states, some large and many small, as measured by area, population or wealth. Each measure has its shortcomings but is so well known as to be used with confidence. What is not available is a measure of something less tangible, the political status of a country. An attempt is made here to do just that by simply adding up for each African country the number of other African states with a permanent diplomatic mission in residence in that country. The greater the number of other African states represented, the higher the status accorded to that country by its own continent. The measure is simple, the statistical source is readily available over time. It could be extended and refined, but here the simple form will suffice.

There is some correlation between diplomatic representation and the number of contiguous neighbours a state has. Peripheral states show up badly and island states suffer from isolation. Size and wealth strongly influence the political pecking order although interestingly the large peripheral island of Madagascar ranks lower than Gambia.

In 1981 Nigeria and Zaire had the greatest political status, followed by Algeria, Egypt, Ethiopia and Senegal. Nigeria's size in population and wealth, and its central location in relation to the continent as a whole is supported by its outward-looking attitude and its conscious assumption of leadership. The growth of Nigerian national confidence through the 1970s is matched by a rise in political status by this measure and its reciprocal, the number of Nigerian diplomatic missions in other African countries. Zaire is large, central and has a large contiguity factor: all nine neighbouring states, except Angola, are represented. Algeria and Egypt are both large states long active in the international politics of Africa.

Ethiopia and Senegal are less obvious candidates for high political status. In this respect Ethiopia owes much to the role of 'elder statesman of Africa' assumed by Emperor Haile Selassie in the 1960s. Anachronistic figure though he was even then, he was able to use his personal charisma, and American finance, to attract to Addis Ababa the headquarters of several important African international organizations, not least the OAU itself and the influential Economic Commission for Africa (ECA). In effect he made Addis Ababa the continental capital where the OAU met more frequently than anywhere else, six times between 1963 and 1973. Before the 1974 revolution Ethiopia ranked highest in political status. The Mengistu government has been, often of necessity, more inward-looking. Senegal's high status must be explained in terms of Dakar's

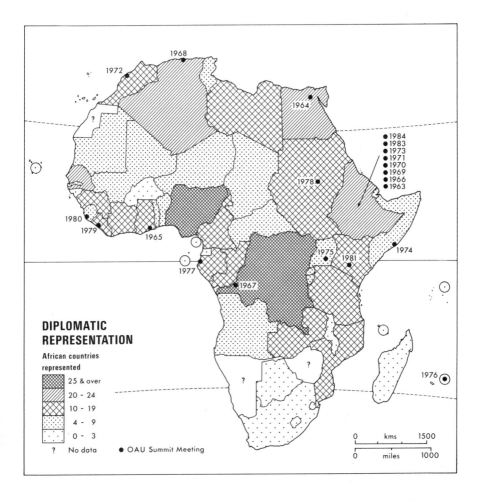

DIPLOMATIC REPRESENTATION

African countries represented

- 25 & over
- 20 - 24
- 10 - 19
- 4 - 9
- 0 - 3
- ? No data
- ● OAU Summit Meeting

0   kms   1500
0   miles   1000

former role as capital of French West Africa (AOF). It is interesting that it has endured so long after independence against competition within Francophone Africa from the more centrally placed Ivory Coast.

The next rank of states contains few surprises except possibly Gabon, whose wealth obviously counts greatly, and Libya whose wealth and aggression have not yet fully paid off in status terms. The status of Gabon, Libya and Zambia has increased markedly over the decade. Zambia has become more central within black Africa as the 'front-line' has moved southwards. The lowest rank in the pecking order contains all six island states and the states of southern Africa. South Africa, the pariah state of the continent, has only one African diplomatic mission in residence, that of Malawi.

59

20 Africa must unite!

'The necessity to guard against neo-colonialism and balkanization, both of which would impede unity' in Africa was long foreseen, but few heeded the Pan-Africanist call of Kwame Nkrumah, 'Africa must unite!'. Some did, unsuccessfully, oppose the division of the French colonial federations in the late 1950s. Léopold Senghor even led Senegal into pre-independence union with the French Soudan as the Federation of Mali, but it broke up after just two months of independence. Julius Nyerere, also unsuccessfully, suggested his own Tanganyika delay independence to keep step with Uganda and Kenya to further the cause of East African unity. The colonial territorial strait-jacket remained intact.

The British had long seen the need for larger territorial units in southern Africa, but theirs was an imperialistic concept and their two creations became vehicles for maintaining white minority rule. The Union of South Africa, set up in 1910, united four colonies into a single, large, rich and strong state, ironically for Africa the only such state to be so created.

Elsewhere the union of colonies into a single state did little to strengthen that state. Eritrea gave to Ethiopia a coastline but also a twenty-year secessionist war. Morocco reunited from 1956 was led to ambitions for Western Sahara and is now being drained by war waged since 1976 by the POLISARIO in the desert and at OAU conference tables. Unification of British and Italian Somaliland in 1960 took Somalis so near their irredentist ideal that it has been their costly obsession ever since. In the union of Tanganyika and Zanzibar as Tanzania in 1964 both parts have gone mostly their own way.

Once independence was separately achieved the task of uniting African states became virtually impossible. Nkrumah, long an active Pan-Africanist, saw the need for unity very clearly and in 1960 led Ghana into the 'Union of African States' with Guinea and Mali which he hoped 'Would prove to be the successful pilot scheme to lead eventually to full continental unity'. But opposition came from states which were 'jealous of their sovereignty and tended to exaggerate their separatism'. In 1961 the African states, though fundamentally sharing similar aims of 'some kind of unity', divided according to the means of achieving it. The Casablanca group, including Ghana, put political unity first, the Monrovia group attached priority to economic associations. By the time the OAU was set up in 1963, the Monrovia group had won decisively.

The impulsive proclamations of unity between Libya and her neighbours by Gadafy have led to nothing except a strengthening of border defences. Unity,

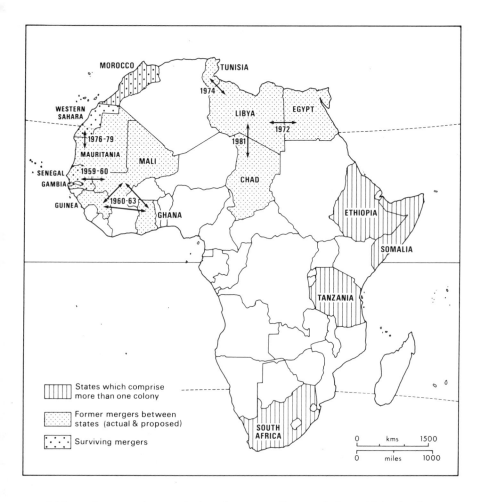

States which comprise
more than one colony

Former mergers between
states (actual & proposed)

Surviving mergers

which can be strength, must be based on mutually agreed aims which take time
to work out and even longer to implement. Even the well-set-up East African
Community (EAC) was smashed on the rocks of regional economic policy,
conflicting ideologies and Idi Amin. Could unity come from some other form of
big brotherliness? The Gambian *coup* of July 1981 was defeated with Senegalese
help. By December both states had agreed to unite as Senegambia from 1
January 1982. The union has geographical logic and its progress will be followed
with much interest. Egypt and the Sudan also seem to be moving effectively
towards a union of great potential.

21 Libya and neighbours

In February 1983 world media reported that a planned *coup d'état* in the Sudan had been thwarted by American alertness. Behind the alleged *coup* stood Colonel Gadafy of Libya. The plot included an air drop of mercenaries to coincide with Libyan bombing of strategic targets around Khartoum and a rising of Sudanese dissidents. To counter the threat, the US sent AWAC surveillance planes to give early warning of Libyan air strikes, and despatched an aircraft-carrier to the Gulf of Sirte. The plot, another of Gadafy's destabilization schemes, had failed thanks to the vigilance of the US. On 13 March 1983 the *Observer* of London carried a story headlined 'How a US plot to trap Libya failed', which claimed that Libya had been set up by the US in 'a classic counter-intelligence operation' which attempted to lure the Libyans into an ambush. Both versions are credible, probably neither is the whole truth. That either might be true says much for the reputation Gadafy has gained since coming to power in a *coup d'état* in 1969, but also for the attitude of the Reagan administration for whom the gadfly Gadafy has become, out of all reasonable proportions, a bogeyman.

Libya is the richest state in Africa in terms of per capita income, with large oil resources and a small population. Gadafy is a radical Muslim leader in whose eyes western politicians eagerly see the gleam of fanaticism. He is erratic and tends to blow very hot and very cold. On separate occasions he has announced the union of Libya with Egypt (1973), Tunisia (1974), Chad (1981) and Morocco (1984), and at different times he has tried to destabilize the governments of all four. Gadafy is an arch-meddler in the affairs of his neighbours. His interventions are not always well considered, as when he sent troops to help fellow Muslim Amin in Uganda, or consistent where Libya supports radical non-Muslim Ethiopia against Muslim Somalia and also against radical Muslim Eritrea.

Gadafy's expansionism in Chad in 1981–2 and apparent French willingness to concede all but *l'Tchad Utile* alarmed Nigeria who mobilized support in the OAU. Gadafy withdrew except from the uranium-rich Aouzou strip, but in mid-1983 again invaded Chad on behalf of ex-president Oueddi Goukouni. The French, anxious not to offend oil-rich Libya were reluctant to support actively the Habré regime but under pressure from conservative Franco-phone African leaders and the United States committed a considerable force. In contrast, apparently eager to confront Gadafy, the US rushed AWACs and anti-aircraft missiles to Chad and a carrier force to the Gulf of Sirte. Libya's intervention coincided with the *coup d'état* in Upper Volta (Burkina Faso) which brought

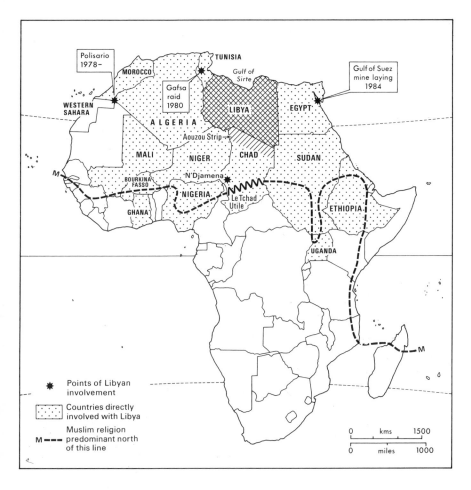

Points of Libyan
involvement

Countries directly
involved with Libya

M --- Muslim religion
predominant north
of this line

the pro-Gadafy Captain Sankara to power, thus concerning the west about the emergence of a radical axis from Tripoli to Accra. Stalemate in northern Chad resulted in an agreement in September 1984 for mutual withdrawal which France honoured but Libya did not.

The POLISARIO issue twice prevented the OAU meeting in Tripoli in 1982 and so Gadafy was not elected to its presidency. Despite a sound, small but well-endowed power base Gadafy has so far failed to achieve lasting influence largely because of his unpredictability. The London Bureau episode and the laying of mines in the Red Sea contrast with the new detente with Morocco as examples of Gadafy's erratic behaviour in 1984 alone. The Soviet Union is a wary ally as Gadafy cannot be relied upon to follow a policy line.

63

22 Senegambia

It is extremely difficult for anyone to appreciate the facts, circumstances, and necessities of the case unless he is familiar with the geography of the regions in question. . . . The French desire Gambia and we desire the French Settlements. It is for Parliament to consider whether the price asked is equivalent to what we are to give. . . . In 1853 the [Gambia] colony was involved in a war with [local tribes] from which it was extricated by requesting the assistance of the French Colony at Senegal. In 1855 the Colony was again at war with them; in 1861 the same state of things arose, and again the Colony had French help.

(The Earl of Carnarvon, Secretary of State for the Colonies, speech in the House of Lords, 17 February 1876)

Apparently suspicious of French desire, and pressured by Manchester merchants, Parliament did not accept the proposals. The Gambia replete with its twenty British residents and one settlement named after an earlier colonial secretary remained British, completely surrounded on the landward side by French Senegal. In 1960 Senegal became independent but it was not until 1965 that the improbable colony of the Gambia became the even less probable independent state. Tiny in terms of area, population and national income the colonial oddity in shape and enclavity became a state of doubtful economic and political viability, its fine river waterway cut off from its natural hinterland by an absurd political boundary. The Gambia's post-independence history has nevertheless been one of remarkable economic and political stability in stark contrast to the record of larger and richer former British colonies in West Africa. About 80 per cent of the Gambia's exports are derived from groundnuts and the only modern economic development is a tourist trade specializing in package tours for sun-seeking Scandinavians.

Eventual union with Senegal has long been a matter for discussion in the Gambia. Post-independence relations between the two governments have generally been good not least because of the stability in both countries and the rapport established between two long-serving presidents Senghor and Jawara. Co-operation was gently encouraged and in 1973, on a visit to Dakar, Jawara admitted union with Senegal to be 'an inevitable and necessary development'. Throughout the 1970s relations between the two countries improved as successive schemes of co-operation were developed and points of friction eliminated. Developments included the Trans-Gambia Highway and the

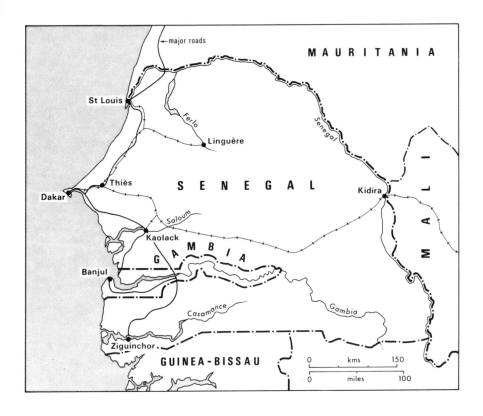

Gambia River Development Organization, both of considerable importance to both states.

In July 1981 Jawara visited London to attend the wedding of the Prince and Princess of Wales. His opponents, taking a leaf from the books of conspirators against Nkrumah, Idris, Obote and Bokassa, staged a *coup d'état* in his absence. Jawara flew to Dakar and, with the assistance of Senghor, fought back. As in 1853 and 1861 Senegal came to the aid of the Gambia against the modern equivalent of warring tribes. Jawara was restored and immediately set about formalizing union with Senegal. On 1 January 1982 the Confederation of Senegambia was formally declared although with little pomp. Since then the work of integration has gone quietly ahead. A confederal cabinet was announced in January 1983, and on 13 January 1983 the first confederal Parliament met at Dakar with 20 Gambian and 40 Senegalese members. Decisions require a 75 per cent majority. Progress towards full union has been painfully slow but this might yet be more effective than rushing headlong into union which could not be sustained.

23 *Coups d'état* and military rule

There have been more *coups d'état* (sixty-two) in post-colonial Africa than there are independent states (fifty-one). Thirty-one states have experienced successful *coups d'état*, fourteen states have had more than one, while Benin and Ghana have each had five *coups*. Twenty-seven states have had military rulers at some time in the post-colonial period, and twenty-two had military rulers at the end of 1982. Eight African leaders have been assassinated in office, from the Abubakar Tafawa Balewa in 1966 to Sadat in 1981, and as many, from Lumumba in 1961, have been murdered or executed following *coups d'état*.

Against these stark statistics of political instability and violence it must be noted that in ten African states the political leader at the time of independence remained in power at the end of 1984. Two of those leaders, Houphouët-Boigny and Nyerere, had each ruled for more than twenty years. Post-1950, the average life-in-office of leaders of independent African states is about seven years, compared with three years for British prime ministers, four years for American presidents and six years for Soviet leaders in the same period.

A *coup d'état*, that in Egypt in 1952 which eventually brought Nasser to power, marked the beginning of the end of colonialism in Africa. But Egypt's revolution did not set the pattern for the spate of *coups* following the great wave of independence which swept black Africa in the years 1957–62. Of the twenty-five states which achieved independence in that period nineteen have since experienced a total of forty-six successful *coups d'état*. Eleven of those states had their first successful *coups* within six years of independence and thirteen have had more than one successful *coup*. In the five years 1965–9 twenty-one *coups* occurred in Africa as a whole, and the number of military rulers rose from one to thirteen. By 1978 there were twenty-two military rulers in Africa and despite some states returning to civilian rule in 1979 the figure rose to twenty-four in 1984 because of further *coups d'état*.

The occurrence of many *coups* soon after independence suggests that the root causes existed at the time of independence. A state such as the Congo (Zaire) was ill-prepared for independence and chaos immediately ensued, its flames fanned by colonial mining interests. But the tragedy of the Congo (Zaire) was the exception rather than the rule. Ten of the new states of 1957–62 experienced their first successful *coups d'état* three to six years after independence. In some, political instability derived from a growing disillusionment with the economic reality of independence. Barely viable colonies made chronically poor states. Riches did not flow and the maldistribution of wealth remained much as before

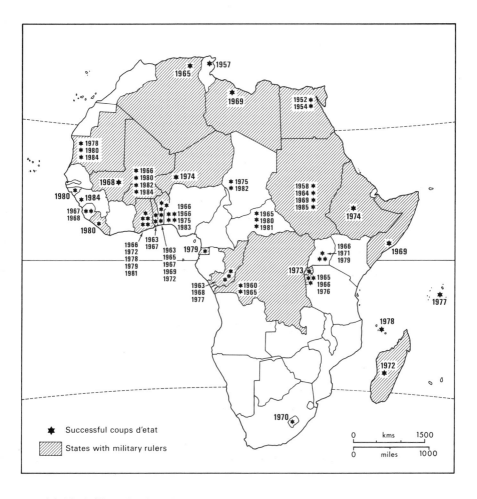

Successful coups d'etat

States with military rulers

with black élites simply substituted for white colonial élites. New governments were often profligate with meagre resources and the cost of the very symbolism of nationhood was frequently excessive. Political power was abused and corruption in high places became a fact of life.

Once the unifying ideal of independence was achieved, compromises and coalitions made in the name of that ideal began to fall apart. Most states had no ideology beyond independence. Carefully arranged checks and balances as between different language groups or different religious groups, between conservatives and progressives, or simply between regions, were difficult to maintain once the colonial power at the fulcrum had removed itself. With the rewards for political success considerable and at the absolute disposal of the government of the day the temptation to seek or retain power by any means including the unconstitutional was overwhelming. On only three occasions since 1950 has power in an African state passed from one civilian government to a different civilian government as the result of an election. Politicians determined on unconstitutional ways of seeking or retaining power naturally enough turned to the military for support. Sometimes this ploy rebounded when civilian *coup* with military support was succeeded by a straightforward military *coup d'état*.

In Uganda the conservative/progressive and regional/ethnic balances created at the time of independence were smashed by Obote in 1966 using a then little-known army commander, Idi Amin. Also in 1966 Nwambutse IV of Burundi was deposed by his son Ntare V, who, before the year was out, was deposed by his military associate Micombero who had assisted in the original *coup*. Except in Morocco and Swaziland all African monarchies and would-be dynasties have been overthrown including those in Tunisia, Uganda and Lesotho where power was originally shared. The three largest states of black Africa, Nigeria, Sudan and Zaire, all fell into civil war with attempted secessions by individual regions distinctive in terms of ethnicity, religion or economic wealth.

The absence of successful *coups d'état* from southern Africa may be related to later dates of independence implying that their turn is yet to come, or it may be that the longer the struggle for independence the more likely is post-independence stability. More persuasive is the argument that the independent states of southern Africa have also faced a constant external threat from adjacent white-minority states, a 'unity bonus' conferred by the status of a front-line state. On the other hand large parts of Angola and Mozambique are occupied by the rebel forces of UNITA and the Mozambique National Resistance (MNR) respectively.

External factors can have a destabilizing effect as in the toppling of the long-established Ould Daddah government (1960–78) in Mauritania. Involvement in the Western Sahara as the accomplice of Morocco rebounded as the POLISARIO attacks disrupted the flow of iron-ore from the Zouerate mines, Mauritania's life-blood. The war, which saw a vast increase in military spending, led directly to a military *coup* which was immediately followed by disengagement, a policy more in line with Mauritania's traditional support of the Saharwis and distrust of Morocco.

For every successful *coup d'état* in Africa there has been at least one unsuccessful one. Former colonial powers have often intervened, to put down attempted *coups* as in Kenya and Tanzania in 1964, or to support *coups* either directly or by instant recognition. It is now embarrassing in France and Britain to recall that Bokassa and Amin, both former colonial NCOs, were quickly and warmly welcomed when they staged their military take-overs. Both became monsters of cruelty, both fell in *coups* themselves, and both were replaced by the very men they had overthrown in the first place. France, through President Giscard d'Estaing, blatantly endorsed the tyrannical excesses of Bokassa, Britain more covertly cosseted Amin long after his brutality was known publicly. In an attempt to extricate himself from an electorally damaging personal scandal Giscard neatly pulled the rug from under Bokassa (but still lost the election). In Uganda Britain stood aside while impoverished Tanzania fought a costly war of liberation against Amin and his Libyan allies. Nyerere may yet pay dearly for the success of his army which in 1982 also held the ring in the Seychelles.

The military are a major force in African government whether or not they actually wield supreme political power in a state. They are coherent, relatively well-disciplined groups able to stand apart from any civilian government heading for trouble. They alone have the arms capability, the independent mobility and logistics often necessary in staging a *coup*. In many cases the military have seen themselves as seizing power to 'clean-up' a civilian mess. They have had a sense of mission which, harnessed to military ruthlessness, has sometimes led to speedy and drastic measures to right perceived wrongs. But there is usually no unifying ideology or even long-term strategy. In office the originally coherent military have often split into factions, resulting in new *coups*. In recent years, military *coup* leaders have sprung from more junior ranks leading to the emergence of more radical forces represented in their very different ways by Colonel Gadafy, Lieutenant-Commander Ratsiraka, Flight-Lieutenant Rawlings, Master-Sergeant Doe and Captain Sankara.

Having seized power the military have not been eager to relinquish it. In only four states is there now a civilian ruler where once there was a military one, though in three others civilian has succeeded military government only to be overthrown again. The year 1979 seemed to be a turning-point marked by the overthrow of Africa's two most grotesque military dictators, Amin and Bokassa, and the return to civilian rule of Nigeria and Ghana. The Ghanaian experiment did not last long before Rawlings again seized power in the midst of chronic economic crisis and charges of corruption against the Limann government. Even earlier, Dacko's second administration in the Central African Republic (CAR) succumbed to a new military *coup*. The Ugandan experience has been to return to a *déjà vu* knife's edge of violence and chaos under Obote.

Bolstered by oil-based wealth the Shagari government in Nigeria cautiously found its feet. But in 1983 it faced an oil glut requiring severe economic readjustment and a general election. The election campaign highlighted the rottenness of civilian politics in Nigeria. Accusations of corruption and ballot rigging were backed by court cases. Shagari was returned but only briefly before a new *coup* brought to power a military government dedicated to cleaning up the mess allegedly created by civilian maladministration.

24 Uganda: from Obote to Obote

Uganda, Buganda, Baganda, Muganda, Luganda: state, kingdom, people, person, language. A liturgy to confuse the outsider who is likely to be further bemused to learn that the kingdom (Buganda) is not the state (Uganda). To grasp fully the last statement is to hold the key to any understanding of the problems of modern Uganda, problems which have reduced one of the most sophisticated societies in Africa to near-barbarism and one of the richest agricultural economies to near-subsistence level.

The roots lie in the colonial period but the deadly flowering of Uganda's problems since independence was by no means inevitable, any more than was the brutality ordinary Ugandans have suffered. Nor can the whole catalogue of horror be laid at the door of one man, Idi Amin. Others, politicians, civil servants, soldiers, policemen, political party thugs; corrupt, greedy, ruthless, cruel men are also unhappily culpable.

The basic British recipe for Uganda was:

Introduce an alien sectarian religion to combat another alien religion, then extend imperial protection
Administer several kingdoms and other tribal areas as one, ignoring political, economic, social, ethnic, linguistic and cultural differences but
Add a little Lugard, apostle of indirect rule, to conserve as much traditional local authority as consistent with imperial protection
Bring the whole to independence, taking care to season with complex constitutional checks and balances
Leave to simmer.

Speke's 'discovery' of the source of the Nile in 1862 opened the way to European penetration. Stanley's letter to the *Daily Telegraph* from Buganda in 1875 read:

Now where is there in all the pagan world a more promising field for a mission than Uganda? . . . I assure you that in one year you will have more converts to Christianity than all other missionaries united can number.

Who could resist such eloquence? Not the Anglicans who arrived hot-foot in 1877 followed, despite protests, by French Catholics in 1879. They vied with each other and with the Muslims for the Kabaka's favours. Confusion increased when in 1884 Mutesa died to be succeeded by his sodomite teenage son, Mwanga. A reign of terror, the most awful violence and bloodshed, ensued.

Many Christian Baganda, Anglican and Catholic, were martyred in appalling circumstances.

Lugard arrived in December 1890 and lived precariously before eventually establishing British 'protection' and extending it to the neighbouring kingdoms. Even in these early days of colonial rule most of the ingredients of modern Uganda's problems were already present. They were to survive as dangerous undercurrents through the colonial period to surface at independence.

Uganda became independent in October 1962 after a troubled preparation. The trouble arose from conflict between forces within Uganda which could be loosely characterized as traditional and modern, and which found their strengths of expression in different regions. The traditional/modern divide was also a south/north divide and an ethnic, linguistic and cultural divide. Traditional

7I

power was associated with Buganda, the largest, most prosperous and most powerful of the old Bantu kingdoms, and its hereditary ruler, the Kabaka. Modern power was vested in the new political party which commanded majority support in the country as a whole but not in Buganda, the Uganda Peoples' Congress (UPC) led by a northerner (Langi) Milton Apolo Obote.

There was no question of Uganda being subdivided or of a united East Africa emerging with reasonable time-span. So a cleverly contrived constitution of careful checks and balances was produced. Within a federal structure which gave considerable autonomy to Buganda, the Kabaka Mutesa II was to be president and the elected majority party leader, Obote, the executive prime minister. It lasted less than four years. In May 1966 Obote used the army to move against the Kabaka who escaped to lifelong exile. The checks and balances were rudely swept aside by an army which was largely northern-based led by a northerner from West Nile district, Idi Amin.

Obote became executive president under a new constitution. He consolidated his hold on the army and strengthened it and introduced more radical measures for Ugandan development. He also devoted time to the wider issues of East African unity and to African and Commonwealth affairs. While away at the Commonwealth Prime Ministers' Conference at Singapore in February 1971 Obote was deposed. A military *coup* led by Idi Amin succeeded with limited bloodshed. The new regime was recognized by Britain with indecent haste perhaps not unrelated to Obote's own *coup* of 1966 and the criticism he was currently voicing of the new British Conservative government's attitude towards arms sales to South Africa. Obote's fall was also welcomed in Buganda even though Amin was a northerner and a Muslim. The tunes soon changed.

In 1972 Amin began to expel all Ugandan Asians. As they had to go to Britain his honeymoon with British government and press abruptly ended. But Amin became an African folk hero, even president of the OAU. That too was short-lived as he systematically eliminated all opposition within Uganda with frightening brutality. In a new reign of terror virtually a whole élite disappeared, either into exile or just disappeared. Thousands were killed, their bodies thrown into the Nile or Lake Victoria, or simply dumped in a forest off the Kampala–Jinja road. The economy began to disintegrate helped by drought in the north. With increasing religious overtones Amin acquired a Palestinian bodyguard and a Libyan military force. Uganda even produced another Christian martyr in the person of Archbishop Luwom. Amin's delusions of grandeur grew and, among other manifestations, found expression in a desire to expand Uganda's territory.

Uganda's boundary with Tanzania was in dispute where the British and Germans had agreed a straight-line boundary which cut across the Kagera river leaving a large piece of territory north of the river in Tanzania and a much smaller piece of territory south of the river in Uganda, respectively known as the Kagera salient and triangle. Each had traditionally been part of the other's territory as the Kagera river is a natural divide. Amin attacked the Kagera salient to 'restore' Ugandan rule. Somewhat to his surprise the Tanzanians hit back and did not stop at the boundary parallel.

From the outset Julius Nyerere had been implacably opposed to Amin and his regime. A personal friend of Obote he had given him political asylum and had encouraged other Ugandan exiles in Dar es Salaam. As Amin's excesses took their toll on Uganda Nyerere determined to intervene. The Kagera dispute triggered a well-prepared position. The Ugandan army was in disarray from continuous purges and lack of supplies deriving from the economic crisis. At the critical moment Kenya cut Uganda's link with the sea and oil supplies. Amin turned to Libya for more support. Gadafy sent troops but to no avail. Amin fled the country, first to Libya and then to Saudi Arabia. The Libyan troops were forced home and the Tanzanians held Uganda.

A provisional civilian government was formed under Youssef Lule, former vice-chancellor of Makerere University, but did not last long. He was succeeded by Godfrey Binaisa who was ousted before elections in late 1980, Uganda's first since independence. The outcome was the return to power of Milton Obote. The economy was in total disarray, law and order was broken down, there was severe drought in Karamoja and the remnants of Amin's army rampaged about the country. Instead of getting off to a fresh start Uganda was plunged into the reawakened memories of the 1966 *coup*. Despite the presence of Commonwealth observers the election result was disputed and many apparent irregularities were never adequately explained. Dissident groups took to arms and their presence in Buganda was used as an excuse for violent excesses by an army which was increasingly ill-disciplined and beyond Obote's control. A series of independent reports culminating in the Amnesty International Report of 1985 declared conditions in Uganda worse than under Amin. Amnesty reported hundreds of thousands killed since Obote's return to power. Refugees streamed out of Uganda to the consternation of neighbouring states, notably the Sudan.

Nyerere's efforts in ridding Uganda of Amin were undone by his eagerness to reinstate Obote who arouses all the former divisiveness and seems unable to cope with the formidable task of government. As with Amin the troubles of Uganda are not all of Obote's making but if any impact is to be made on the corruption, violence and brutality which have become daily currency in Uganda a strong disciplined lead is needed. Things might improve if the economy can be restored but that possibility is sabotaged by the very conditions referred to. In 1970–80 GNP per capita in Uganda fell in real terms by 4.1 per cent per annum, or more than one-third overall. The state of Uganda is not a happy one, a fact all the more tragic because of what it was and could be again.

25 Congo/Katanga to Zaire/Shaba

The Congo (Zaire) was the African colony probably least prepared for the independence received from Belgium, the colonial power least prepared to accept its new status. The immediate result was a chaos of terror and brutality which underlined the fragility of African independence, exposed the forces of neo-colonialism and emphasized the dangers of national disintegration through provincial secession. Also, for the second time in recent history the Congo caused Africa to become the board on which international rivalries of non-African powers could be played out in comparative safety to those powers.

The crisis in the Congo was complex in its causes and convoluted in its course. Political development was rudimentary, recent and regionally based. Lumumba from Stanleyville (Kisangani), the most radical and most widely supported leader, emerged as prime minister and Kasavabu, the Bakongo leader, as president. Independence came on 30 June 1960 in an atmosphere of distrust between the new government and Belgium.

On 5 July sections of the Congolese army (*Force Publique*) mutinied against its Belgian officers (there were no Congolese officers). As violence spread Europeans fled the country. Lumumba dismissed the Belgian army commander and on 8 July appointed Mobutu army chief of staff as Belgian paratroops flew in to protect Belgian citizens and property. On 11 July Katanga (Shaba) was declared independent by its leader Tsombe. Lumumba appealed to the UN, Ghana and the Soviet Union for help and a UN-led international operation was mounted to enable the Congo to survive as an integral state.

The Congolese army put down another attempted secession in Kasai but failed to make any impression on Katanga where Tsombe was able to deploy a white mercenary-officered army through strong financial backing from Belgian business interests, mainly the large mining corporation *Union Minière du Haut Katanga*. In September 1960 Lumumba and Kasavubu fell out, tried to dismiss each other but were both dismissed by Mobutu in an army *coup d'état*. Lumumba escaped, was recaptured, and eventually murdered in January 1961.

UN resolve to reunite the Congo was strengthened but it took two years more and the life of Secretary-General Hammarskjöld to achieve. Civilian rule returned under Adoula but further rebellion broke out at Stanleyville, Lumumba's former power-base. Mobutu ousted Adoula and invited Tsombe to the Congo premiership. Katangan forces with the aid of Belgian and American paratroops put down the rebellion. Tsombe's usefulness over, Mobutu staged a second *coup* and has ruled ever since.

74

Under Mobutu the Congo gained relative stability though heavily dependent on American support freely given to keep out the Russians and to secure strategic mineral supplies. Apart from an extreme bout of 'traditionalism' in the early 1970s the Mobutu regime has had no guiding ideology. Relations with post-independence Angola have been strained as Zaire was used as a base for American-backed *Frente Nacional de Libertacao de Angola* (FNLA) guerrillas. In 1977 exiled Katangans invaded Shaba from Angola and were repulsed only by Franco-Moroccan intervention. When the invasion was repeated in 1978 Kolwezi was taken and again the French intervened, this time with Belgian support. The Mobutu regime drifts in a sea of corrupt incompetence unable to defend itself, propped up by the United States and France who are intent on safeguarding their own political and economic interests.

26 Nigeria

Nigeria's emergence as a major political force in Africa has three basic foundations: it is the most populous state in Africa, it has the largest economy of any black African state and, having come through a baptism of fire, remains a single state.

Controversy surrounds the detailed enumeration of Nigeria's population. As it had been announced before the first post-independence census in 1963 that the population count for each state would form the basis for allocation of parliamentary seats, a political premium was placed on generous head-counting. The 1963 census gave a total population of 55.7 million, hotly disputed as far too high because of regional inflation of the figures. A second census in 1973 recorded 79.8 million, in contrast to the UN mid-year estimate for 1973 of 59.7 million, and was officially set aside. In 1978 the Federal Election Commission estimated a population of 78.5 million compared with the UN mid-year estimate for 1979 of 74.6 million. Whatever the detailed figures there is no doubt that Nigeria is by far the most populous state in Africa.

Such a large population in Africa inevitably means enormous ethno-linguistic diversity. There are 395 languages of Nigeria, strictly defined as languages and not dialects. Three languages dominate: *Hausa*, an Afro-Asiatic language spoken across much of northern Nigeria, *Yoruba* in the south-west of the Niger–Kordofarian family of languages and, of the same group, *Igbo* which, with closely related *Igala*, is largest in the south-east. Between north and south the 'middle belt' is fragmented into literally dozens of separate languages in a cultural buffer zone. A similar but smaller phenomenon occurs between south-west and south-east. Along the eastern boundary zone from the Niger delta to Lake Chad there is also considerable ethno-linguistic diversity. The critical translation from diversity to divisiveness comes not so much from the high degree of fragmentation as from the existence of three regionally dominant language groups. Religion is a second cultural divide in Nigeria: the north is predominantly Muslim, the south is not. The British practised indirect rule in the north reinforcing the power and Islamic conservatism of the Emirs. Christian missions had a major impact in southern Nigeria, not least in education leading to a westernization and modernization of attitudes which contrasted strongly with the traditionalism of the north.

The Nigerian economy, the largest in Africa in 1980, was overtaken by that of South Africa in 1981. Traditionally based on a broad range of agricultural, mineral and industrial products and a long history of internal and international

trading, since 1970 the economy has been dominated by oil. In 1980 oil accounted for 96 per cent of Nigerian exports, 25 per cent of GDP, and 85 per cent of government revenue. Nigeria is an apparent contradiction in terms, a rich developing country, but its prosperity and development hopes are vulnerable because they are dependent on a single wasting resource exported as a crude raw material and subject to price fluctuations beyond domestic control.

Nigerian oil resources are vast, about 3 per cent of known world reserves. Nigeria is the largest oil producer in Africa and ninth largest in the world. The oilfields are in the Niger delta, both on-shore and off-shore, exploited by about 150 oil wells the first of which was drilled in 1956–7. Production throughout the 1960s was modest, 10–20 million tonnes per annum, but rose rapidly from 1969 to peak at 111.6 million tonnes in 1974. Thereafter until the world oil glut of the late 1970s production was pegged at about 100 million tonnes per annum.

Nigerian crude oil is high quality, very light and low in sulphur and, with Algerian, Libyan and North Sea oil, commands the highest prices. Nigeria exported vast quantities of crude oil only to import refined products for domestic consumption until mid-1980 when the third Nigerian refinery at Kaduna (5 million tonnes per annum capacity), with the earlier refineries at Port Harcourt (2 million tonnes per annum) and Warri (5 million tonnes per annum) managed to meet all domestic demand. Only about 2 per cent of Nigeria's natural gas production is utilized, the rest being wastefully flared off. Increased internal use of natural gas is planned and also a major investment in a Liquefied Natural Gas (LNG) plant so that the enormous surplus might be exported.

These investment plans and countless others depend on the continuing prosperity of the oil industry. Since 1978 there has been a world glut of oil. The Organization of Petroleum Exporting Countries (OPEC), which Nigeria joined in 1972, has tried to keep prices up by reducing production. Nigerian output fell from 100 million tonnes in 1980, to 70 million tonnes in 1981. As a developing country, and one that had been profligate in the use of its new-found wealth, Nigeria was more vulnerable than most OPEC members. OPEC recognized this and in 1982 allowed Nigeria to retain its reduced production ceiling of 64 million tonnes whilst all other members had their quotas further reduced. But despite price reductions oil sales plummeted. OPEC showed a great sympathy and restraint as Nigeria's desperation threatened an all-out price war, narrowly averted in March 1983 but even more likely in October 1984.

Falling oil revenues had, in mid-1982, forced the Nigerian government to suspend all imports in an attempt to ease a major balance of payments crisis. In April 1983 Nigeria was forced to renegotiate large current trading account debts, and talks were held with the International Monetary Fund (IMF). The Nigerian financial crisis demonstrated the dangers of overwhelming dependence on a single raw material commodity, even when that commodity was oil. Development and economic diversification are long and costly processes not helped, in the case of Nigeria, by over-ambitious plans and extravagant spending at all levels of government. Although severe the crisis has not yet undermined Nigeria's long-term prospects, provided that lessons have been learned and that economic and moral self-discipline is asserted.

Oil was also an ingredient in Nigeria's baptism of fire: the civil war and attempted secession of Biafra. The constitutional history of Nigeria before and after independence reflects concern with the feasibility of creating a unified state while balancing the regional interests of north, west and east, Hausa, Yoruba and Ibo. In the run-up to independence in 1960, the emphasis was not so much on speed as on finding an appropriate constitutional formula. The federal constitution was a compromise solution under which the regions delegated to the centre certain powers including the vitally important control of army, police, customs and excise, currency, central banking and regulation of international trade. As the arguments developed the principal political parties in Nigeria became increasingly regionally based and all, at some time, threatened secession.

At independence the federal government was a coalition between north and east. It did not last long. A political split in the west led the federal government to take over the regional administration, eventually to install in power the minority group aligned with the north and to create a new Mid-West region. The 1963 census and the 1964 federal election strained north–east relations and the east was strengthened by its growing oil production. In January 1966 a pro-Ibo army *coup* killed the federal prime minister, Balewa, and the regional leaders of north and west. The new military leader, General Ironsi, proclaimed a military state but in July, after anti-Ibo riots in the north, he was overthrown in a new anti-Ibo *coup* that installed Colonel Gowon. Reconciliation failed as more riots in the north killed thousands of Ibo resident there. In July 1967 the Ibo east declared the independent state of Biafra and the Nigerian civil war began. After an initial Ibo advance through the mid-west region had been repulsed, the military outcome was never in doubt. The tragedy was that the federal forces were unable to end the affair quickly because outside powers, including France, Portugal and South Africa, sustained Biafra until it dwindled to not much more than a single airstrip. Thousands of innocent civilians died and many more suffered severely from a war that lasted two and a half years.

The Federation of Nigeria survived intact, reconciliation began, and because of the astonishing expansion of oil production at a time of rising oil prices a strong and rich state emerged from a sea of colonial balkanization and political and economic weakness. Despite some successes the Gowon government began to drift and was overthrown in a bloodless *coup* in July 1975. The new leader, General Murtala Muhammed, was vigorous and efficient, dealing with long-standing problems and detailing a timetable for return to civilian rule. But in February 1976 he was assassinated. Government passed peacefully to General Obasanjo with maximum continuity of purpose and in 1979 civilian rule was restored. Shehu Shagari was elected to a new American-type, executive presidency with a fixed four-year period of office, to face a difficult baptism as the basis of the Nigerian economy was assailed in the oil-glut crisis. He also faced the problems of a society where the riches derived from oil were enjoyed by the few who flaunted and squandered their wealth and where corruption and graft dominated the political and commercial scene. New elections in August 1983 returned Shagari to power but not without violence and deaths in Ibadan and allegations of ballot rigging in Ondo and Anambra states, which were subsequently upheld by the courts. On 31 December 1983 the army stepped in once more to overthrow the government, allegedly to clean up the mess of civilian maladministration.

Despite all efforts to submerge regional differences the parties in the 1983 elections still reflected the former tripartite division of north, east and west. The

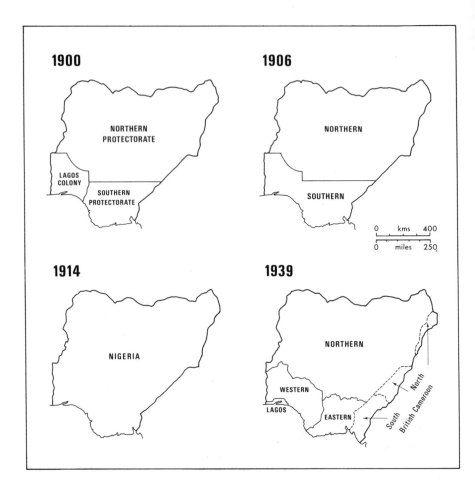

British had set up a unitary administration in Nigeria in 1914 but in 1939 created the three regions which survived independence. The Mid-West region was created in 1963 and, to allay fears of domination by any one region, the number of regions or states was increased to twelve in 1967, and nineteen in 1976, plus Lagos and the new Federal Capital Territory. The new states do not represent a radical geographical restructuring but successive sub-divisions of the three 'parent' regions. This probably does less to overcome the old divisions than if the new states cut across the basic tripartite regional boundaries and could not be so easily identified as being part of the old north, east or west.

The new capital city, 'Abuja the symbol of our unity', is taking shape having been formally opened in 1982, when it was little more than an extensive building

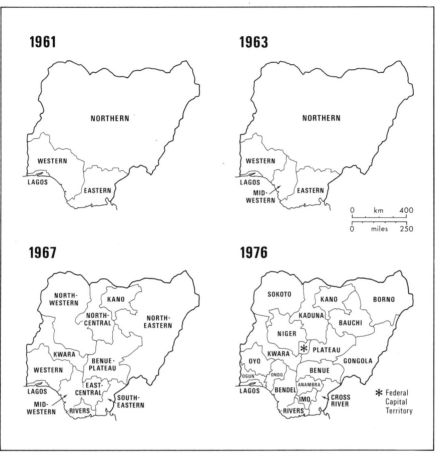

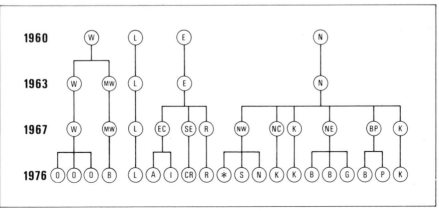

site. About 300 miles (500 km) north-east of Lagos, Abuja is near the geographical centre of Nigeria in the 'middle belt'. It is hoped Abuja will help ease the chronic congestion of colonial Lagos and get Nigeria off to a new independent start. The cost of the project is startling, £800 million to the end of 1982, £2400 million by 1986, though the oil crisis must now delay fulfilment of plans. Projected population of Abuja is in excess of 1.5 million.

Despite the cost in lives and resources there is little doubt that the interests of all Nigerians and all Africa were best served by the preservation of a strong, dynamic and united Nigeria. Future strength depends on the ability to adjust to the new, lower level of prosperity induced by the oil crisis. The economic boom had produced its own problems of social discipline, wasteful spending, corruption and a high crime rate. Oil helped to divide Nigeria in the late 1960s, oil was the very basis of Nigerian economic and political recovery from a particularly nasty civil war and so became the means of re-asserting national unity in the 1970s. The oil crisis of the 1980s could even help Nigeria better to achieve its vast potential.

27 Somali irredentism

Somalia is one of Africa's poorest countries yet it has chosen for much of its existence to sacrifice economic progress for the ideal of Somali self-determination. While other African states have struggled to create national unity from groups of diverse ethnic origin, language and religion, Somalia has been absorbed with its aim of uniting all Somali people in a 'Greater Somalia'. Somalia's aim and the total rejection of that aim by the neighbouring states with Somali minorities is an intractable problem exacerbated by the strategic position of the Horn of Africa which has attracted the attention of imperial powers for more than a century. Thousands have been killed in the warfare that has punctuated the post-colonial period, thousands more have died from related causes, and up to 1.5 million Somalis have become refugees.

At independence in 1960 Somalia was already a rarity in Africa, a union of two colonies, British Somaliland (68,000 square miles/174,000 sq. km; 650,000 people) and Italian Somaliland (178,000 square miles/456,000 sq. km; 1,230,000 people). Even then nearly 1 million Somalis lived outside the Somali Republic, occupying areas of Ethiopia, Kenya and French Somaliland (Djibouti) totalling about 128,000 square miles (328,000 sq. km). Roughly one-third of all Somali people and one-third of all land occupied by Somali people lay outside the Somali Republic.

About 70 per cent of Somalis are pastoral nomads who manage to eke out a precarious living from a harsh, semi-arid environment. The seasonal and longer-term migratory patterns of such a people present a dynamic force inevitably at odds with fixed international boundaries, especially so when those frontiers are arbitrarily drawn straight lines. For over a century Somalis are known to have migrated steadily westward across north-eastern Kenya displacing other groups as they moved. Northern Somalis have also migrated westwards into Djibouti. Each year the Somali/Ethiopian boundary in the Ogaden is ignored by herdsmen following the rains to fresh pastures in fairly well-defined seasonal migrations.

Both Somali colonies were administered by Britain during and after the Second World War. In 1946 a British proposal to create a 'Greater Somalia' of the two colonies plus the British-occupied Ogaden was rejected by the United States and the Soviet Union who were suspicious of British ambitions in the strategic Horn. In 1950 the Italians were handed back their colony as a UN trust territory, and five years later Ethiopia was allowed to reoccupy the Ogaden.

In 1924 Britain had transferred the greater part of the Jubaland province of

Kenya, an area of 36,740 square miles (94,050 sq. km) entirely inhabited by Somalis, to Italy who subsequently added it to her Somaliland colony. This transfer was motivated solely by the need to 'reward' Italy for her efforts in the First World War and to compensate for Britain and France acquiring former German colonies elsewhere in Africa. It was no attempt to solve the Somali minority problem, 14,000 square miles (35,800 sq. km) of Somali-inhabited Jubaland remained in Kenya, and the Somalis were also spread more widely over Kenya's Northern Province. No part of Kenya was included in the proposed 'Greater Somalia' of 1946.

Between the independence of Somalia in 1960 and that of Kenya in 1963, Britain was pressured to cede the remaining Somali areas of Kenya to Somalia. Nothing came of it though a new North Eastern Region was created in 1963 prior to the Anglo–Somali conference at Rome where no agreement was reached as Somalia pressed its claim to the whole of the former Northern Province. In December 1963 Kenya became independent with the 1924 boundary with Somalia intact.

Kenya's original regional system of government, intended to protect Somali, among other minority interests disappeared in the new constitution of 1965. Somalia's hostility intensified into bitter guerrilla war which cost hundreds of lives and brought suffering to the Somali people on both sides of the border but achieved nothing for the cause of Somali self-determination.

That cause was further set back in French Somaliland in 1967 when a referendum, at which the French carefully mobilized the non-Somali vote, declared against independence which many had seen as a first step towards unification with Somalia. The name of the French overseas territory was changed from *Côte Française des Somalis* to *Territoire Français des Afars et des Issas*, a more accurate if more cumbersome title, but perhaps also one truly indicative of French political intentions.

The super-powers, having blocked British plans for Somalia, were not long in establishing themselves in the strategic Horn. In return for a Red Sea base the United States provided Haile Selassie with the arms to keep his fragile Ethiopian empire together. The Soviet Union outbid the west to give Somalia military aid in return for a base at Berbera. Between them the superpowers armed Ethiopia and Somalia with modern weaponry which was employed in sporadic warfare between the two countries in the early 1960s.

Late in 1967 Prime Minister Egal's new Somali government recognized the impoverishing effect and apparent futility of pursuing self-determination and attempted to negotiate a settlement with Kenya and Ethiopia. The guerrilla war died out and Somalia was, almost for the first time, at peace with its neighbours. Ironically the removal of the unifying external issue led to internal political strife culminating in the military *coup* of 1969 which brought Siad Barre to power.

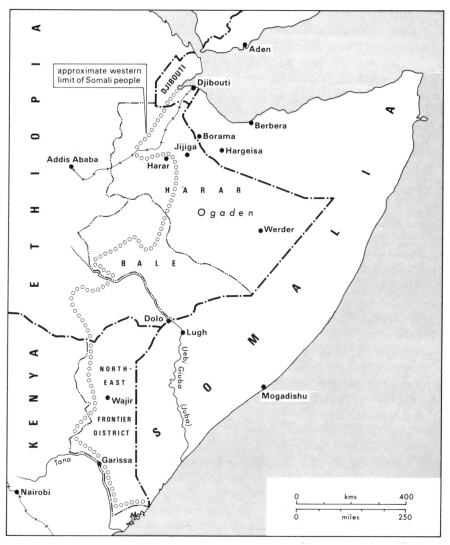

approximate western
limit of Somali people

0	kms	400
0	miles	250

Egal's policy was continued, with emphasis placed on the formidable internal development problems of Somalia. But the Ethiopian *coup* of 1974 and the blaze of publicity which accompanied Siad Barre's OAU chairmanship once more raised Somali hopes of self-determination. The Soviet Union, Somalia's superpower ally, now also replaced the United States in the counsels of Ethiopia and attempted, without success, to mediate between the two sides on the self-determination issue.

85

Somalia moved to take advantage of the chaos in Ethiopia. In the Ogaden the Western Somali Liberation Front was formed with Somalia's support and by the latter half of 1977 full-scale war was in progress. The Somalis were initially highly successful around Harar but in March 1978 the regrouped Ethiopian army, equipped by the Russians and 'advised' by 15,000 Cubans, inflicted a crushing defeat on the Somalis at Jijiga. The formal war was virtually over but intensive Somali guerrilla activity continued, matched by border incursions and air raids by the Ethiopians, with occasional Somali army forays into the Ogaden leading to inconclusive pitched battles as at Werder in August 1980.

The war coincided with serious drought to drive the Ogaden Somalis from their traditional pastures. Over 800,000 fled eventually to be housed in refugee camps set up by international relief organizations and the UN on the Somali–Ogaden borders. Food supplies were often insecure and health hazards multiplied with the drought. Each flare-up of the war caused an upsurge in refugee numbers and impeded relief work. A UN estimate of early 1981 put the refugee numbers as high as 1.5 million.

Siad's government was threatened by the severe drain on Somalia's meagre resources and by political discontent. The guerrilla war eased and by 1982 Ethiopian forces were secure in the Ogaden. Refugees attempted to resume their lives as pastoral nomads and the worst seemed to be over. Then in mid-1982 there were sustained attacks from the Ogaden on Somali forces from the Ethiopian army or, as the Ethiopians claimed, from Somali dissidents. The United States, an unenthusiastic supporter of Somalia, began to ship arms into Mogadishu. But tension eased and armed clashes became less frequent against a background of political manoeuvre in Mogadishu and another drought gripping the Ogaden.

The Ethiopian revolution fanned the flame of Somali irredentism. Unable to restrain Somalia or resist the temptation to move into Ethiopia the Russians became deeply involved. In supporting Ethiopia in maintaining the boundary status quo they took the only course acceptable to the OAU but paid the price of expulsion from Somalia and American occupation of the Berbera base. The balance of the early 1970s gave way to instability as the superpowers moved to opposite ends of the Horn's see-saw. In 1983 the United States' rift with Ethiopia seemed to be ending and the Soviet presence seemed to depend on the prolongation of conflict on Ethiopia's periphery.

The basic Somali problem remains unsolved. The two superpowers prevented an early solution in 1946 and have since exploited Somali aspirations and Ethiopian disarray for their own perceived strategic advantages. The chances of negotiated settlement are extremely slim as no political leader in Ethiopia or Kenya could realistically contemplate transferring tracts of land to Somalia, and in the long term Somalia will not be satisfied with anything less. As long as

Ethiopia and Kenya remain strong superpower clients there is little Somalia can do to further self-determination for the Somali minorities. Were they to weaken Somalia would be tempted to try again. The outlook is bleak unless Somalia, Kenya and Ethiopia could be encouraged to plan jointly the development of the interior Somali lands. They are desperately poor, ravaged by periodic drought and badly in need of improvement. Initiative and material assistance would have to come from outside as the lands are peripheral to the larger states and low on their scale of priorities. The rewards could be more than simply economic because development co-operation could possibly lead to lasting political accommodation.

28 Ethiopia and Eritrea

For more than twenty years a bitter and costly war has been fought in Eritrea with no peaceful settlement in sight. Ethiopia regards the conflict as a secessionist war waged by a rebellious region which, if successful, would leave Ethiopia land-locked, and in danger of further disintegration. The Eritreans see the conflict as a fight for the basic human right of self-determination denied them in the past by the UN. They do not regard Eritrea as a part of Ethiopia but as a separate political entity which was forced into federation and then union with Ethiopia. The two positions are irreconcilable as long as Ethiopia believes in a military solution and so war goes on, wasteful of human life and scarce resources.

Eritrea contains within its colonially drawn boundaries a wide diversity of landscapes, peoples and cultures. It comprises a narrow coastal strip along the Red Sea over 600 miles (1000 km) long which widens out in the north to include a high plateau extension of the Ethiopian highlands and beyond that a western lowland bordering the Sudan. *Tigrinya* speakers, who live on the plateau, make up about half the total population of Eritrea and are mainly Christians who share their language and religion with their neighbours in the Tigre province of Ethiopia. *Tigre* speakers of the western lowland and the northern coastal strip make up about one-third of the population and are Muslim. In the southern coastal strip the *Danakil* are Muslim nomadic herdsmen related to the *Afar* of neighbouring Djibouti. Other small language groups in the north are mainly Muslim but with Christian minorities. In general, the coastal and western lowlands are inhabited mainly by Muslims, the plateau mainly by Christians.

Eritrea knew no unity before the Italian occupation, different parts at different times owing allegiance to different surrounding empires. From the sixteenth century the western lowland and northern coastal strip were part of the Ottoman Turkish empire, which was succeeded in the nineteenth century by Egypt, in turn succeeded by the Mahdist state. Ethiopia held the allegiance of the high plateau area but until the nineteenth century showed little interest in the coast, being for most of recent history a land-locked Christian empire dependent on its highland base for isolated survival surrounded by Islam.

Eritrea was the creation of the European scramble for Africa. The ports of Assab and Massawa became Italian colonies in 1882 and 1885 respectively, and in 1890 they were incorporated into an Italian colony which included the whole coastal strip between British Sudan and French Somaliland. The boundaries of the new colony were drawn by Europeans, even the name Eritrea (Erythrea) was derived from the classical name for the Red Sea. The Italians then claimed a

'protectorate' over Ethiopia but were soundly beaten by the Ethiopians at Adowa in 1896. They retreated to Eritrea to brood over their defeat for forty years. In that period Eritrea was, for the first time, welded into a single political entity with unified political and social structures which cut across traditional divisions as happened in all other European colonies in Africa and which, in a vast majority of cases, formed the basis for eventual independence.

Under Mussolini a modern Italian army conquered Ethiopia and held it until thrown out by British Commonwealth troops, mainly South Africans, five years later. Between 1936 and 1941 as part of the Italian East African Empire Eritrea and Ethiopia were for the first time ruled together. In 1941 Eritrea was placed under British military administration while Ethiopia regained her independence. After the war Eritrea's future status had to be decided, like that of other Italian colonies but not Ethiopia, by a Four Power Commission of Britain, France, the Soviet Union and the United States.

The Four Power Commission failed to agree on Eritrea's future, having four different proposals: union with Ethiopia (Britain), partition with the highlands and southern coastal strip going to Ethiopia (United States), trust territory with Italian administration (France) and trust territory with international administration (Soviet Union). The problem passed to the UN who set up a Commission of Burma, Guatemala, Norway, Pakistan and South Africa which was also divided. They rejected partition outright, Guatemala and Pakistan proposed UN trusteeship leading to independence, but the majority favoured close association with Ethiopia. Burma and South Africa suggested federation with some autonomy, Norway wanted full union. The United States backed federation and with only nine votes against (including the Soviet Union) UN Resolution 390A of December 1950 was passed. From September 1951 Eritrea was to become an autonomous territory federated with Ethiopia. The preamble to the resolution refers to Ethiopian claims to Eritrea 'based on geographical, historical, ethnic or economic reasons, including in particular Ethiopia's legitimate need for adequate access to the sea'. It also desired the federation 'to assure the inhabitants of Eritrea the fullest respect and safeguards for their institutions, traditions, religions and languages as well as the widest possible measure of self-government'.

The disparate views of the two commissions reflected the diversity of opinion within Eritrea but also the self-interest of the powers involved. In Eritrea a Unionist party based in the highlands, and an 'Independence Bloc' of parties broadly favouring independence, had emerged. Ethiopia, allowed great latitude to influence affairs in Eritrea by Britain, financed the Unionists and intimidated the Independence Bloc with a terrorist campaign against its leaders and supporters. Ethiopia was also active diplomatically, most effectively with the United States which favoured the concept of a strong Ethiopian ally occupying a strategic seaboard and this was decisive. The 1953 Defence Pact between the United States and Ethiopia completed the deal, and America replaced Britain as military supplier and adviser to Ethiopia. British sources at the time were of the opinion that a majority of Eritreans would have voted for independence.

Ethiopia abused the terms of the UN resolution and systematically set about turning federation into union. *Tigrinya* was replaced by *Amharic* as the official language and the 'autonomous' government was blatantly interfered with. Elections were held without the safeguard of UN supervision, a puppet government was installed and political harassment of those who favoured independence for Eritrea continued. As a result the Eritrean assembly voted for union with Ethiopia but before it was effected fighting began.

The absorption of Eritrea into Ethiopia aroused little international attention as the matter was considered internal to Ethiopia which at this time commanded considerable prestige. Haile Selassie ruled through an oppressive feudal system at home but his autocratic style impressed in international affairs. In the first decade of African independence he was able to emerge as a father figure, the African emperor who had triumphed over colonialism, whose pride and dignity had shamed the conniving politicians of pre-war Britain, France and the whole League of Nations. He secured for Addis Ababa the headquarters of the UN Economic Commission for Africa (1958) and the OAU (1963) and with them an endorsement for his government and its works.

The war in Eritrea escalated into fully-fledged guerrilla warfare and massive retaliation. Almost inevitably the Eritreans divided, the more radical Eritrean People's Liberation Front (EPLF) challenging the Eritrean Liberation Front (ELF) and both indulging in internecine warfare. The Eritreans in general were represented as left-wing Muslim dissidents who, by attacking conservative Christian Ethiopia, undermined United States strategy centred on the survival of Israel. But when the Ethiopian revolution of 1974 installed a neo-Marxist government in Addis Ababa that dismissed the United States as Ethiopia's chief patron and turned to the Soviet Union, the Eritrean situation did not essentially change. By the end of 1977 the Eritreans gained control of all the territory, except for some garrison towns, but, instead of negotiating, the Mengistu regime, now backed by the Soviet Union and Cuba, sought a military solution. In 1978 an Ethiopian army of over 100,000 with Cuban and Russian support was launched and eventually retook most of Eritrea at considerable cost. Thousands of Eritreans were killed and hundreds of thousands of refugees fled into the Sudan. Since then a 'fluid-stalemate' has been reached where Ethiopia is unable to eliminate Eritrean guerrillas and the Eritreans are unable to establish themselves.

The intractable Eritrean problem abounds with ironies. The Soviet Union, supporter of Eritrean independence in 1950, is now chief accomplice in a brutal war. Cuba, who helped train Eritrean guerrillas in the 1960s, now has 15,000 troops in Ethiopia supporting the Mengistu regime. The United States, against Eritrean independence in 1950 but dismissed by Ethiopia in the 1970s, is still anxious not to offend the Mengistu regime as it hopes to regain its lost position in Ethiopia. Libya and Yemen are prepared to let a radical Muslim liberation movement suffer in order to ally with non-Muslim Ethiopia against the Sudan and other conservative Arab states. Saudi Arabia and other conservative Arab states are cautious about dealing with the EPLF, preferring the ELF, and are therefore in danger of splitting the Eritreans even further. The OAU, hopelessly split over another liberation movement in Western Sahara, chooses to ignore Eritrea as a problem internal to Ethiopia. Heads or tails the Eritreans seemingly cannot win and are the victims of cynical manoeuvring by powers who apparently have a total disregard for human life and values. Meanwhile rebels in the northern province of Tigre have taken to arms to demand greater autonomy from the decaying empire of Ethiopia.

Eritrea and Tigre were badly hit by the droughts of 1983–5 with thousands dying but the wars continued relentlessly. The Ethiopian government indicated its own priorities by refusing international aid access to the drought-stricken war zones, by giving arms precedence over grain shipments, by channelling food aid to its own army and by airlifting Tigreans to forced resettlement in southern Ethiopia. Emergency food aid for Eritrea and Tigre has had to be routed through the Sudan in convoys which run the gauntlet of Ethiopian MiG aircraft attack. The Ethiopians even seized a shipment of grain from Australia bound for Eritrea via Port Sudan at Assab. To escape war and famine tens of thousands of refugees have streamed across the Sudanese border to relief camps where very basic food supplies are available.

After twenty-four years the Eritrean war cannot be won yet it drags on. It represents imperialism, African imperialism, at its worst. The Ethiopian Empire, ruled by a Marxist–Leninist regime, is like an onion. The outer skins of Eritrea, Tigre and the Ogaden are peeling away. The world sheds tears at the widespread human suffering, tries to treat the symptoms but does nothing about the causes. Ethiopia could not continue the war without Soviet arms supplies but should the Soviets refuse the Dergue would turn to the United States for military aid and, sadly, would probably receive it. No effective pressure is brought to bear on the Dergue. There is room for compromise in Tigre because the Tigreans do not even seek complete autonomy. The Eritrean problem is more difficult but not impossible. For example, Ethiopia could allow Eritrean self-determination in return for Eritrean recognition of Assab and the southern Danakil coast as part of Ethiopia. In this way Ethiopia would not become land-locked, one of the fears expressed in the 1950s. An unwinnable war could end, the killing could cease, meagre resources could be concentrated on overcoming poverty and easing human suffering. There can be no point in continuing to force such a union as that of Ethiopia and Eritrea even though in principle in Africa larger, more viable states are desirable. The forced union of Ethiopia and Eritrea has been totally self-defeating.

29 Western Sahara

The Western Sahara problem is essentially similar to that of Eritrea. On ceasing to be a European colony Western Sahara was occupied by a neighbouring African state claiming historic rights. The territory is also of considerable present-day value to the occupying power. The people of Western Sahara have been denied the right of self-determination and their nationalist organization is deadlocked in a guerrilla war against a powerful state which has superpower support. In its details, and in its impact on the rest of Africa, the Western Sahara problem is very different indeed from that of Eritrea.

In 1884 Spain claimed the 600 mile (1000 km) Saharan coast between Morocco and Mauritania as its 'sphere of influence'. Spanish enthusiasm for the Sahara was limited to this foggy desert coast which faced their valued possession of the Canary Islands. Although France became dominant in Morocco, Spain secured those parts strategically important to it; the northern Rif, facing Spain itself, and the hinterland to Ceuta and Melilla; the southern protectorate opposite the Canary Islands and contiguous with Western Sahara; and the port enclave of Sidi Ifni. Spanish interest in and control over the interior was minimal. It is desert except in the north where limited winter rainfall supports sparse scrub vegetation. The population is small, mainly nomadic herders whose traditional territories extend beyond the mainly straight-line political boundaries of today. The Spanish census of 1974 put the total population of Western Sahara at 73,500 but the UN estimates 200,000 persons. Minerals changed Spain's disinterestedness. In 1965 deposits of 1700 million tonnes of high quality phosphates were confirmed at Bu Craa. A phosphate refinery was built there with a trunk conveyor to El Aaiun. As many had anticipated for some time, Western Sahara was suddenly transformed from a desert wasteland to a valuable piece of real estate. Phosphates are of particular interest to Morocco which is the only other major phosphate producer outside the United States and the Soviet Union and is the world's largest exporter.

After attaining independence in 1956, Morocco was aggressively expansionist and claimed Western Sahara, Mauritania and parts of Algeria on the basis of the sixteenth-century Moroccan empire which had extended as far as Timbuctoo. In 1957 Moroccan forces invaded Western Sahara but were repulsed by Spanish troops. After Algerian independence war flared between Morocco and Algeria in 1963 over the boundary which had been in dispute in colonial times. The conflict centred on the Tindouf area which contains large, unworked deposits of iron-ore. The Moroccans were again repulsed. Diplomacy took over and was more effective. Spain gave up Ifni to Morocco in 1968 leaving the issues of Ceuta and Melilla and Western Sahara to be resolved. Morocco and Algeria signed a treaty of friendship in 1969 and Morocco recognized Mauritania so relinquishing her territorial claims on that state. Morocco continued to call for the decolonization of Western Sahara on the assumption that Spain's withdrawal would be followed by Moroccan rule. But Spain's belated phosphates-led interest in Western Sahara resulted in some economic and political development. In 1967 Spain set up the Yema'a, an assembly of nominated and elected members to give advice on matters of local administration. In 1973 the Yema'a asked that Saharans be allowed self-determination and in 1974, to Morocco's consternation, Spain agreed in principle. Meanwhile in May 1973 a new nationalist movement, the POLISARIO front, had been formed to accelerate political development by direct action.

The advent of the POLISARIO galvanized Morocco into diplomatic action. The UN was persuaded to ask the International Court of Justice to advise on the legal status of Western Sahara before Spanish colonization. It also agreed to a UN mission to assess the problem on the spot and to visit other interested states. Spain meanwhile agreed to postpone a referendum in Western Sahara until the UN had received both reports. Late in 1974 Morocco and Mauritania secretly agreed to partition Western Sahara between them when the opportunity arose.

In mid-October 1975 things came to a head dramatically when within a few days of each other the UN mission and the International Court of Justice published their findings as Franco lay dying in Spain. Both reports recognized pre-colonial ties between Western Sahara and Morocco, and Western Sahara and Mauritania, but saw no reason to withhold from Saharans the right of self-determination. Spain, playing for time, went back to the UN who suggested a six-month cooling-off period. King Hassan replied on 6 November 1975 by leading 350,000 Moroccans in the 'Green March' across the Saharan border. On 14 November an agreement was signed between Spain, Morocco and Mauritania. By early 1976 Spain had withdrawn leaving Western Sahara partitioned between Morocco and Mauritania, with Morocco occupying the northern two-thirds including the Bu Craa mines.

Ignored in the take-over the POLISARIO fought on and, in February 1976, set up the Saharan Arab Democratic Republic (SADR). With help from Algeria, including effective sanctuary, the POLISARIO first chipped away at Mauritania whose vital iron-ore mine at Zouerate and railway to Nouadhibou could not be easily defended, even with French airforce help (1976–8), against guerrilla attack. The unpopular war which threatened the main national resource, drained the fragile economy and built up the army, all for little worthwhile gain, resulted in a military *coup*. In 1978 the Ould Daddah government fell, a cease-fire followed, and in 1979 Mauritania concluded a peace treaty with SADR.

94

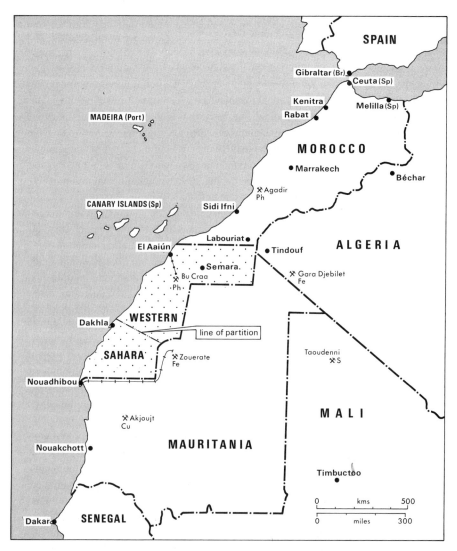

The war between the POLISARIO and Morocco settled into stalemate. The
POLISARIO controlled three-quarters of the territory but Morocco held the
part that matters economically – the Bu Craa, El Aaiun, Semara triangle. The
POLISARIO intermittently attack Moroccan defences in this area and in
southern Morocco around Labouriat, but do not break through well-prepared
positions protected by sophisticated equipment supplied to Morocco by the
United States which has a military base at Kenitra.

On the diplomatic front the POLISARIO/SADR steadily gained support and recognition. A majority of African states were ready to admit SADR to membership of the OAU at the 1980 Sierra Leone summit. But a vote was avoided and the issue referred to a committee which bought time but no acceptable solution as its recommendations were turned down by Morocco in 1981. In February 1982 at an OAU ministerial meeting at Addis Ababa SADR was admitted by a simple majority. The decision was controversial as supporters of Morocco claimed the meeting inquorate since fewer than two-thirds of all delegates were present. In March SADR delegates were refused permission to land at Dakar for an OAU information ministers' meeting so other delegates walked out. Later that month Moroccan delegates and those from seven other countries left an OAU Labour conference at Harare because SADR was seated. In August 1982 the OAU summit at Tripoli could not be held because more than one-third of member states stayed away, incidentally preventing the election of President Gadafy as chairman.

The Western Sahara problem was stalemated. Militarily the POLISARIO could only irritate the entrenched Moroccans but they would not go away and as long as they had a safe base in Algeria they could not be decisively beaten. Any diplomatic solution required a referendum as the OAU proposed in 1981, but Morocco would not accept prior withdrawal and the POLISARIO/SADR would not accept a referendum while Morocco was in control of the Saharan towns. An apparently simple question of self-determination had got caught up in the interwoven webs of African, Arab and superpower politics. The OAU was openly split into conservative and radical camps in a stunning and damaging display of African disunity, divided not necessarily on the merits of the problem but according to traditional loyalties, political prejudice and self-interest.

Morocco's African supporters, including Senegal, Somalia, Tunisia and Zaire, wanted the status quo maintained fearing that a POLISARIO victory would strengthen radical forces in the OAU. Saudi Arabia and the United States shared these concerns on wider fronts and were prepared to support Morocco with financial aid, military supplies and diplomatic influence. The POLISARIO/SADR could not have survived without Algerian sanctuary. Algeria was alarmed at Moroccan expansionism but also wanted access to the sea via El Aaiun to develop the iron-ore deposits near Tindouf. Libya had been a fitful SADR supporter partly because Algeria had not been enthusiastic to embrace the erratic Gadafy. Other African supporters of SADR include Ethiopia, Angola, Mozambique and Zimbabwe. The Soviet Union had a long-term agreement over phosphates with Morocco but allowed the POLISARIO to be equipped with Russian arms including SAM7 missiles.

Recent developments in the Western Sahara saga have been complex and distinctly contradictory. In April 1983 Morocco and Algeria began to patch up their differences and for the first time in almost eight years opened the border between them. The draining effects of the war on the one side and falling oil revenues on the other encouraged mutual co-operation. In late 1984 Libya and Morocco announced that after an official visit by Gadafy to Rabat the two countries were to unite to further the cause of Arab unity. The quid pro quo for Gadafy's recognition of Morocco's position in the Western Sahara was Hassan's recognition of Libya's position in northern Chad. That their two staunchest allies were making up their quarrels with Morocco did not seem to help the cause of the POLISARIO/SADR. Yet at the OAU summit of June 1984 the POLISARIO/SADR had been seated as full members for the first time and Morocco had responded by walking out.

In the final analysis the *de facto* position in Western Sahara is what matters. The Moroccan army has gradually pushed out its wall of sand to form a line of defence several hundred miles long effectively protecting the economically important northern part of Western Sahara. Topped with radar installations the wall prevents the POLISARIO from continuing their earlier devastating surprise strikes. They are now free to roam at will only through the sandy wastes of the south or to hurl themselves against the expanding defensive wall in costly routine attacks. Behind the wall large new iron ore deposits of high quality have been identified and Morocco is planning their exploitation. The diplomatic success of the POLISARIO/SADR at the OAU for the moment seems to be a hollow victory because on the ground things appear very much to favour Morocco. Another form of African imperialism is apparently succeeding, grabbing land and rich mineral resources whilst denying the Saharans the right to self-determination.

30 Angola

Angola's independence, assured by Portugal's revolution of 1974, was not achieved until 11 November 1975. By then Angola was gripped by civil war between three rival liberation groups each backed by foreign troops. Cubans and South Africans, proxies for the Soviet Union and the United States respectively, are still in Angola. Their continued presence is bound up with the issue of independence in Namibia. Until that is settled the Angolan government is not secure enough to dispense with the Cubans but the South Africans see Cuban withdrawal as a pre-condition for Namibian independence.

An accord between the rival liberation groups broke down in March 1975 when the FNLA, based among the northern Bakongo people and assisted by Zairean army units and mercenaries, attacked the *Movimento Popular de Libertacao de Angola* (MPLA), a largely urban-based radical group among detribalized *assimilados* and mulattos in and around Luanda. From the south UNITA, based among the Ovibundu people, also fought the MPLA. Both FNLA and UNITA were backed by the United States and the MPLA by the Soviet Union. On 23 October 1975 South Africa invaded and rapidly took Mocamedes, Lobito and N'gunza. Cuban troops and Soviet arms were rushed to Luanda to reinforce Soviet-equipped Cubans already 'advising' the MPLA. Despite airlifts of US arms the FNLA were forced back to the Zaire border. The South Africans were held at the Cuvo river 250 miles (400 km) south of Luanda.

South African intervention was self-defeating. It justified the MPLA's use of Cubans and induced hitherto uncommitted African states, led by Nigeria on 27 November 1975, to recognize formally the MPLA as the Angolan government. By February 1976 the US House of Representatives, seeing the spectre of Vietnam over Angola, had voted against Kissinger's policy; the OAU had recognized the MPLA government, and the South Africans had withdrawn to create a cordon sanitaire against SWAPO guerillas north of the Namibian border.

Since 1976 the South Africans have frequently struck into Angola, notably in December 1983 when 2000 troops with air support penetrated over 125 miles (200 km) killing over 500 SWAPO guerillas. This incursion coincided with a major offensive launched by UNITA which since independence has, sustained by South Africa, controlled the south-eastern quadrant of Angola. In early 1984 UNITA advanced across the Benguela railway, which it has managed to keep closed since 1975, to attack the Lucapa diamond mines. They also advanced

over the high plateau areas around Huambo and Malanje. In 1985 the invasion
of the diamond fields was repeated with a similar sorry group of ex-patriot
mining technicians being forced to march out of Angola via the 'Savimbi trail'.
The blows rained on SWAPO tighten South Africa's grip on Namibia. The
continued closure of the Benguela railway denies the MPLA much needed
revenue and enforces greater SADCC dependence on South African rail routes.
By linking it with Cuban withdrawal from Angola, South Africa has gained
enormous scope for procrastination on Namibian independence. These are parts
of the same total strategy for the survival of white-minority rule in South Africa.
An added bonus would be if the MPLA was to fall or at least was forced to do
a deal with UNITA.

31 Zimbabwe

The fight for independence in Zimbabwe was finally won more than fifteen years after Zimbabwe's former partners in federation had obtained their independence. Yet Zimbabwe immediately faced three daunting problems: land, tribalism and South Africa.

Rhodes's pioneer column of 1890 was in search of another Witwatersrand which failed to materialize so that land became Rhodesia's main attraction. Land, someone else's land, was a currency the British South Africa Company could afford. By 1899 16 million acres (6.3 million ha) had been alienated and pressures on the land soon built up. European land increased steadily although much of it was unoccupied and undeveloped, held to ensure future European occupation. In 1971 the Rhodesia Front regime contrived a land apportionment of 44.95 million acres (18 million ha) each to Europeans and Africans. At the time Africans outnumbered Europeans by 21 to 1 (5.3 million to 0.25 million), a greater proportion of Africans were dependent on the land, and much African land was infertile and remote. Population growth itself is a major factor in the land problem in Zimbabwe for in this century the African population has grown twelve-fold. Land was symbolic in the independence struggle but independence has not solved the problem. Zimbabwe needs the commercial production of European farms but also has to face the legitimate aspirations of its people for land. The key land issue is a political tightrope along which little progress has been made leaving many frustrated people prey to other disaffections.

Tribal differences blighted the independence struggle and were exploited by successive settler regimes. About 80 per cent of Zimbabweans are Mashona and 15 per cent Ndebele. Past relationships between the two groups were complex but tribal rivalry is still present. The post-independence period has seen the problem intensify, exacerbated by land hunger: arms finds in Matabeleland and threatened insurrection, the sacking of Nkomo from the cabinet, kidnapping, accusations of impending imposition of a one-party state, the arrest of Nkomo, the rampage of the army's 5th Brigade through Matabeleland, Nkomo's flight plus the charge against Nkomo and his supporters of collaboration with South Africa.

South Africa is not an imaginary external threat posed to promote internal cohesion in Zimbabwe. It was always an economic threat to Rhodesia which tried to develop independently behind tariff walls. Rhodesia refused a direct railway connection with South Africa until Mozambique's independence in 1975. The constellation of states policy is a blueprint for South African economic

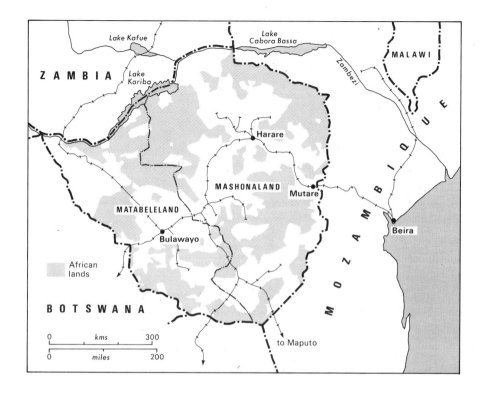

hegemony and would be resisted by Zimbabwe even were it advocated by Buthelezi rather than Botha. Zimbabwe's route to Beira has been sabotaged by Mozambique National Resistance (MNR) guerrillas and the destruction of oil installations at Beira in December 1982 and subsequent attacks on the pipeline have hurt the Zimbabwean economy, and forced the government to negotiate for oil supplies via South Africa. Oil, the one strategic mineral it lacks, is something South Africa would dearly like to be seen supplying to Zimbabwe. South Africa backs the MNR, is directly involved in acts of sabotage in Mozambique, and has admitted to cross-border incidents in Zimbabwe itself. Most of all South Africa would like to induce Zimbabwe to enter into a mutual non-aggression pact similar to the Nkomati Accord with Mozambique.

Mugabe's tightrope is a high wire and he has a long way to go to overcome the major problem of land, let alone withstand external pressures and contain internal dissension. The attempt to create a one-party state is absorbing much effort. The means used could well be counterproductive and the effort expended probably could be put to more effective use elsewhere among Zimbabwe's many problems.

32 The French connection

In 1973 the then finance minister of France, Giscard d'Estaing, accepted the gift of a package of diamonds from Bokassa, the military dictator of the Central African Republic. In 1977 Bokassa crowned himself emperor in a vulgar ceremony which vainly attempted to recreate the splendour of Napoleon's French empire. In 1979 in Operation Barracuda Giscard sent 1000 French paratroopers to overthrow Bokassa and reinstall Dacko his predecessor in office. These episodes epitomize in exaggerated form France's relationship with post-colonial Africa: French economic exploitation particularly of minerals, cultural links based on the French heritage, and military intervention to safeguard French interests. At its worst the French connection is blatant neo-colonialism but because they are interested, active and positive in Africa French excesses are generally tolerated and they 'get away with' things no other power would even try, such as supplying South Africa with a US $1000 million nuclear power complex, and Mirage fighter-bombers, directly until 1977 and since then for local manufacture under licence.

French influence in Africa is based on twenty former French colonies and three Indian Ocean territories which remain French. Francophone influence also extends to the three former Belgian colonies of Zaire, Rwanda and Burundi and to two former British colonies, Mauritius and the Seychelles, which are largely bilingual (English and French) having passed from France to Britain in the colonial period. Thirteen African states are members of the Franc Zone and have currencies linked to the French franc at a fixed rate of exchange and freely convertible into French francs. Financial reserves are held mainly in French francs and exchange is arranged through the French money market. For most Franc Zone countries in Africa France is the main trading partner especially for imports which are mainly manufactured goods. Exports are largely raw materials, often minerals. The trading relationship which is very much in France's favour provides an economic rationale for the maintenance of French interest in Africa.

Military involvement is perhaps the most distinctive part of the French relationship with Africa. All the Francophone states, except Guinea, have military assistance or defence agreements with France. There are French bases in Djibouti, Gabon, Ivory Coast and Senegal with a total of about 6000 French troops plus about 1500 stationed in the Central African Republic. French military intervention was frequent in the early days of African independence and again during the Presidency of Giscard d'Estaing when French troops were

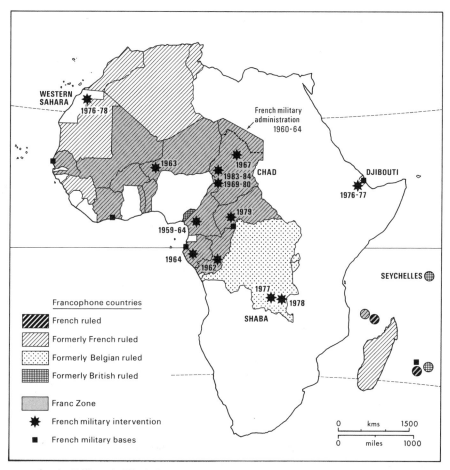

Map legend:

Francophone countries
- French ruled
- Formerly French ruled
- Formerly Belgian ruled
- Formerly British ruled
- Franc Zone
- French military intervention
- French military bases

Map labels: WESTERN SAHARA 1976-78; French military administration 1960-64; 1963; 1967 1983-84 1969-80; CHAD; DJIBOUTI 1976-77; 1979; 1959-64; 1964; 1962; 1977; 1978; SHABA; SEYCHELLES

Scale: 0 kms 1500; 0 miles 1000

active in Djibouti, Chad, Mauritania (Western Sahara), Zaire and the Central African Republic. The French have almost invariably helped maintain the status quo, often at the request of threatened African governments.

The French-led suppression of the Shaba rebellions of 1977 and 1978 in Zaire showed the spread of French influence which remains strongest in Ivory Coast, Senegal, Gabon and Cameroon. That the French connection in Africa will continue is clear though Afro-French relations have suffered through the Chad crisis of 1983-4. In August 1983 French troops were sent to Chad to counter Libyan incursion. When an apparent stalemate was reached France and Libya agreed over the heads of their Chadian clients to withdraw their troops. To President Mitterand's embarrassment, French withdrawal, completed in November 1984, was not matched by the Libyans.

33 Land-locked states

Africa has fourteen land-locked states, more than any other continent including Europe with its rash of surviving medieval 'statelets'. The African land-locked states are in three blocks, west, east and south-central, plus Swaziland and Lesotho:

Mali	Uganda	Malawi	Swaziland	Lesotho
Upper Volta	Rwanda	Zambia		
Niger	Burundi	Zimbabwe		
Chad		Botswana		
CAR				

Most land-locked states were territories least integrated into the colonial systems. In the British case most were indirectly ruled protectorates with Swaziland and Lesotho small African kingdoms which had emerged as such only in the nineteenth century. The lack of colonial interest reflected geographical remoteness but also an awareness that many of these territories had little to offer in the way of resources except perhaps labour. With the obvious exceptions of Zambia and Zimbabwe this is still largely true, and among the land-locked states are some of the smallest and poorest in Africa. Most are weak states, economically and politically; remote backwaters dependent on stronger, richer, more accessible neighbours.

Seven land-locked states were among the eleven poorest states in Africa in 1981. In contrast only one land-locked state, Botswana, was among the twelve richest African states by this measure. Only one land-locked state, Zimbabwe, had a total GNP in excess of US $5000 million in 1981. Only one, Uganda, had a population in excess of 10 million. Land-locked states also came low in the political pecking order with, on average, less than half the number of resident diplomatic missions from other African states than the seaboard states, despite having more direct neighbours or a higher contiguity factor. By most measures of size, wealth and influence the land-locked states, as a group, stood out as being among the weaker states of the continent.

In colonial times most land-locked states were starved of modernization investment. In particular there were few infrastructural improvements so that five of the land-locked states, for example, do not have a single mile of railway, while Lesotho has just that, one solitary mile. The common problem of land-locked states is that of access. Distances to the sea are often great even by the shortest route. The Central African Republic (CAR), Chad and Rwanda are

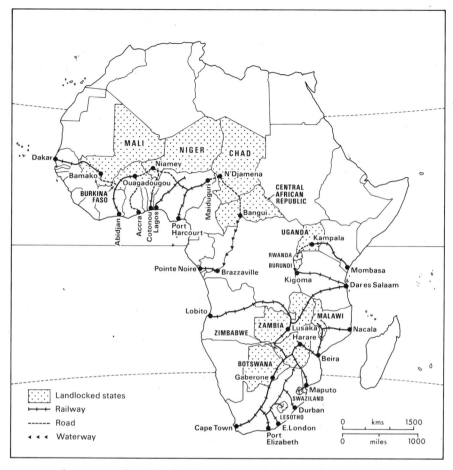

MALI
NIGER
CHAD
Dakar
Niamey
Bamako
Ouagadougou
N'Djamena
BURKINA
FASO
Maiduguri
CENTRAL
AFRICAN
REPUBLIC
Abidjan
Accra
Cotonou
Lagos
Port
Harcourt
Bangui
UGANDA
Kampala
RWANDA
BURUNDI
Pointe Noire
Brazzaville
Mombasa
Kigoma
Dar es Salaam
Lobito
MALAWI
ZAMBIA
ZIMBABWE
Lusaka
Nacala
Harare
BOTSWANA
Beira
Gaberone
Maputo
SWAZILAND
Durban
LESOTHO
Cape Town
E.London
Port
Elizabeth

Landlocked states
Railway
Road
Waterway

kms   1500
miles   1000

more than 1000 miles (1600 km) from the sea by any surface route. Botswana,
Burundi, Mali, Niger, Uganda, Upper Volta and Zambia are all more than 500
miles (800 km) inland.

The traditional colonial access routes were not always the shortest. The all-
French route from the coast to Chad not only is twice as long as the most direct
route but also involves costly trans-shipments between different modes of
transport. It runs from Pointe Noire to Brazzaville by rail, then by river to
Bangui, and thence by road to N'djamena, a distance of over 1800 miles
(2900 km) through three countries. From Port Harcourt by rail or road to
Maiduguri and thence to N'djamena by road is about 1085 miles (1750 km)
through two countries. The route from the Cape to the Zambian copperbelt via
the spinal railway is about 2150 miles (3440 km) compared with the route from

Dar es Salaam of about 1130 miles (1810 km). The new shorter routes have required considerable investment, none more than the Tanzam route which is now followed by oil pipeline, tarred road and railway all completed in 1968–75 after Zambia's independence at a total cost of over £200 million. Other costly post-independence route developments include the Malawi–Nacala rail link, and tarred roads from Rwanda to Uganda, Mali to the Abidjan railway and Upper Volta to Accra. All imposed a considerable financial burden on relatively poor states.

The land-locked state is vulnerable in a way no seaboard state is. It can be threatened by closure of a boundary as between Zambia and Rhodesia intermittently from 1966 to 1979; or less dramatically, between Senegal and Mali in the 1960s. Rhodesia itself became a prey to the same pressure after Mozambique became independent in 1975 and reacted in a similar way to Zambia by building a new railway link to the coast via a friendly state, in this case South Africa across the Limpopo at Beitbridge. The vulnerability of post-independence Zimbabwe and Zambia is demonstrated in another way as rail links to the sea at Beira and Lobito respectively have been disrupted by MNR and UNITA forces backed by South Africa. Rwanda has been vulnerable to communications disruptions by violence and warfare in Uganda through which the only tarred road outlet runs. Almost invariably the states through which access is sought are more powerful than the land-locked states and a dependency can easily develop.

A land-locked state is perhaps most vulnerable when it depends on bulk transport as Zambia does for copper exports where the volume of flow is great and needs to be regular. Issues such as port congestion, railway operating schedules and rolling-stock deployment become vitally important. To sustain a regular flow of traffic to and from a land-locked state requires careful co-ordination and the closest co-operation between transport authorities in all the minutiae of operation and maintenance as well as in the larger matters of investment and route development. This is rarely fully achieved if only because the access states have different priorities for their scarce resources.

Leaders of land-locked states seem to develop a form of geopolitical claustrophobia, the main symptom of which is obsession with routes of access. Their concern is always the availability of alternative routes as the folly of relying on a single route has been underscored time and again. When most people were happy to learn that Kenya had restricted supplies to Uganda in the last months of Amin's regime, leaders of single-access land-locked states probably winced. At Southern Africa Development Co-ordination Conference (SADCC) meetings Zambia has called for yet more alternative routes to the sea. The special continental viewpoint of the land-locked state adds an important psycho-geographical dimension to the geopolitics of African development.

Land-locked State	Capital city	Port	Mode of Transport	Approx. distances miles	km
Botswana	Gaborone	Cape Town	rail	975	1560
		Port Elizabeth	rail	800	1280
		Beira	rail	1065	1705
Burundi	Bujumbura	Dar es Salaam	lake/rail	900	1440
		Matadi	road/river/rail	1825	2920
CAR	Bangui	Pointe Noire	river/rail	1100	1760
Chad	N'djamena	Pointe Noire	road/river/rail	1810	2900
		Douala	road	1175	1880
		Port Harcourt	road	1085	1735
		Lagos	road	1240	1985
Lesotho	Maseru	Durban	rail	390	625
		East London	rail	400	640
Malawi	Lilongwe	Beira	rail	460	735
		Nacala	rail	570	910
Mali	Bamako	Dakar	rail	800	1280
		Abidjan	road	745	1190
Niger	Niamey	Cotonou	road	710	1135
		Accra	road	880	1410
Rwanda	Kigali	Mombasa	road	1035	1655
Swaziland	Mbabane	Maputo	rail	225	360
Uganda	Kampala	Mombasa	rail	725	1160
Upper Volta	Ouagadougou	Abidjan	rail	725	1160
		Accra	road	630	1010
Zambia	Lusaka	Dar es Salaam	rail	1150	1840
		Lobito	rail	1650	2640
		Beira	rail	1245	1990
			road	650	1040
		Port Elizabeth	rail	1765	2825
Zimbabwe	Harare	Beira	rail	375	600
		Maputo	rail	770	1230

34 Africa's strategic 'chokepoints'

Africa, Mackinder's 'southern peninsula', joined to the Eurasian land-mass by the narrow isthmus of Suez, has impeded trade routes between east and west throughout history. The long route around Africa, the Cape sea route, has been of strategic importance to western Europe ever since it was opened up by Vasco da Gama in 1497–8 but its importance has increased significantly since the Second World War. Of equal strategic importance is the Suez canal route. Apart from the 100 mile (160 km) canal itself, the route passes through two long, narrow seas, the Red Sea and the Mediterranean Sea, both of which have very narrow entrances, respectively the Straits of Bab el Mandeb and the Straits of Gibraltar. In modern jargon these straits, the isthmus of Suez and the Cape of Good Hope are strategic 'chokepoints' through which vast quantities of modern shipping are funnelled. At these points the routes are most vulnerable and most need protection. Only the jargon is new for the concept is as old as the routes themselves.

The great modern trade between east and west is in oil. In 1981 the Middle East produced 27.2 per cent of world oil and consumed 2.9 per cent. Western Europe produced 4.6 per cent but consumed 21.5 per cent. Western Europe imported 500 million tonnes in 1981 or 36 per cent of world imports. The Middle East exported 725 million tonnes in 1981 or 51 per cent of world exports. About 75 per cent of western Europe's oil imports come from the Middle East and about 25 per cent of United States imports. All the vast oil trade between east and west passes through one or more of Africa's strategic 'chokepoints' and the same routes also carry large quantities of other cargoes.

The choice of route from the Middle East to western Europe is a matter of weighing the length of the Cape sea route against the restrictions and costs of the Suez canal route. From the Straits of Hormuz at the entrance of the Persian Gulf to the Straits of Dover via the Cape is over 6000 miles (10,000 km) longer than via Suez. Savings in distance and time have to be put against canal charges. But in addition the capacity of the Suez canal is limited in two ways, size of ship and number of transits per day. The canal is deep enough to allow ships of up to 67 feet (20 m) draught to pass through, that is oil tankers of up to about 150,000 deadweight tons (dwt) loaded. The trend in world shipping has been for a greater proportion of tonnage to be in very large tankers. In 1981 36.8 per cent of world tanker capacity was in ships of over 250,000 dwt and another 32 per cent in ships of between 100,000 dwt and 250,000 dwt. Over 50 per cent of world oil tanker capacity was in ships too large to use the Suez canal when laden. The number of

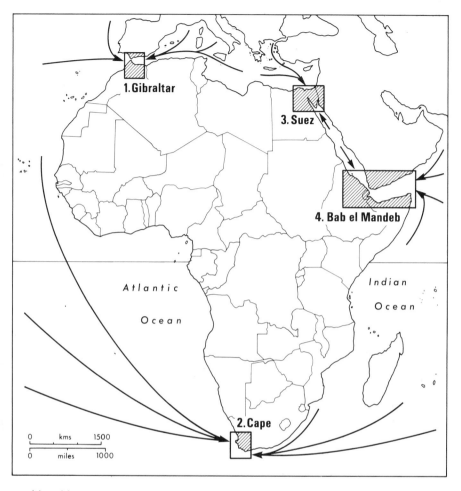

1. Gibraltar

3. Suez

4. Bab el Mandeb

Atlantic

Ocean

Indian

Ocean

2. Cape

| 0 | kms | 1500 |
| 0 | miles | 1000 |

ships able to pass through the canal is also limited to about seventy per day. The combination of ship size and transit restrictions is partly overcome by the Suez–Mediterranean oil pipeline (SUMED) built in 1976 to bypass the canal. The pipeline is 200 miles long (320 km), of twin 42 inch (1.067 m) diameter pipes with a total capacity of 1.6 million barrels of oil per day. Its route south and west of the delta keeps it away from the vulnerable canal.

The Suez canal route passes through a politically sensitive region, the instability of which is enhanced by the canal itself. In the First World War the canal was threatened from the east by Turkish forces; in the Second World War it was the major objective of German troops advancing from the west. Since then the canal has been closed twice because of war and military occupation, from

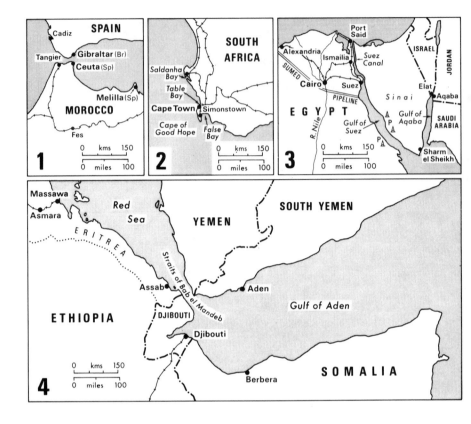

October 1956 to April 1957 and from June 1967 to June 1975. During these periods almost all east–west trade had to be diverted around the Cape.

The Straits of Gibraltar are 12.2 miles (19.5 km) wide between Morocco and Spain. Portugal and Spain have successively held Ceuta since 1415. Britain, as a maritime power aware of the need for strategic naval bases, has held Gibraltar since 1704. Britain also occupied Aden from 1839, a generation before the Suez canal itself was opened in November 1869. The French have been on the other side of Bab el Mandeb since 1859. The modern superpowers also have interests: until 1974 the United States had a defence treaty with Ethiopia while the Soviet Union acquired naval facilities at post-independence Berbera and Aden. From the mid-1970s the superpowers have exchanged positions in Ethiopia and Somalia. The Straits of Bab el Mandeb are 12.5 miles (20 km) wide but at the narrowest part is Perim island held by South Yemen. During the 1973 Israeli–Egyptian conflict guns were placed on Perim island covering the very narrow shipping lanes.

The Cape 'chokepoint' is caused by shipping keeping near the South African coast to minimize distances and to avoid gales further south in the 'Roaring Forties'. Occupied by the Dutch in 1652 the Cape was taken by the British in 1795 for strategic reasons during the Napoleonic wars. Until 1975 the British used the naval base at Simonstown under a defence agreement with South Africa. Elsewhere on the route the United States have a major base at Diego Garcia in the mid-Indian Ocean and use of facilities at Mombasa which are balanced by Soviet access to Maputo and Nacala. In the twelve months July 1981 to June 1982 2453 merchant ships, including 661 tankers, used the Cape sea route. When the Suez canal was closed, and before the world trade recession 14,000 ships a year used the route. It is difficult to exaggerate its importance or to deny how convenient it is for ships using the route to have access to facilities in South African ports, although tankers in excess of 200,000 tons are too large to enter South African ports. It does not necessarily follow that the Cape sea route is likely to be attacked in peacetime, or even in war, or that the route is most vulnerable at the Cape itself. Western powers seem to agree that overt alliance with the present South African government is probably not the best means of defending the route. The Cape sea route is important to the west but the policy implications of its significance are by no means so straightforward.

D Economic

35 Poverty

By any material measure in general the people of Africa are poor. The GNP of fifty-three African territories (the fifty-one independent states plus Namibia and Reunion) added together total about one-eighth the GNP of the United States. Average GNP per capita in Africa is only one-sixteenth that in the United States.

These measures of wealth and poverty, though widely used, need to be handled carefully especially when used on a comparative basis across cultures and continents and in terms of a single currency. Particular problems include the proper assessment of subsistence agriculture, which is the economic activity of the overwhelming majority of Africans; the inability to account for cultural and environmental factors affecting food, clothing, fuel and shelter; the use of a monetary common denominator so that fluctuations in currency exchange rates are sometimes the dominant feature in an index supposed to reflect comparative material well-being; while average GNP per head of population hides possible gross inequalities caused by maldistribution of wealth within societies. Nevertheless there is no getting away from the basic assertion that in material terms Africa is a poor continent.

There is enormous contrast in levels of GNP per capita between countries in Africa. At one end of the scale Libya enjoys a GNP per capita of about one-half the United States level, while at the other, eleven states have a GNP per capita of under US$250 per annum. Libya is very much the exception and only twelve territories in Africa have a GNP per capita in excess of US$1000. Most are well endowed with mineral wealth, especially oil. Libya and Gabon combine rich oil resources with low populations. Algeria has large quantities of oil and gas with a moderately sized population. Nigeria, the largest oil producer is not among the richest states on a per capita basis because of its very large population. South Africa and Namibia have vast mineral resources, and Namibia has a very small population. The Indian Ocean islands are of comparative prosperity, especially the French overseas department of Reunion whose wealth derives from sugar but also from substantial financial support from France in aid and remittances.

The poorest states in Africa are in the Sahel and the Horn. They have few resources and recently have been ravaged by drought. In Chad, Uganda, Ethiopia and Somalia war has taken its toll and there is a direct causal relationship between war and poverty, poverty and war, a vicious, vicious circle of suffering. In fifteen African states GNP per capita fell in real terms over the decade 1973–82, in Uganda by over 4 per cent per annum.

Maldistribution of wealth within a state is perhaps best illustrated in South

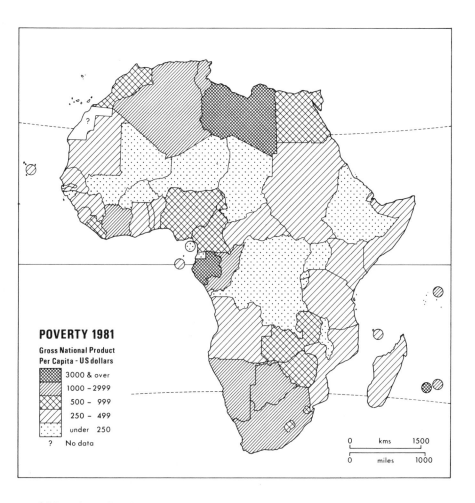

POVERTY 1981

Gross National Product
Per Capita - US dollars

- 3000 & over
- 1000 - 2999
- 500 - 999
- 250 - 499
- under 250
- ? No data

```
0        kms      1500
0        miles    1000
```

Africa where the white population enjoys standards of living at least comparable with the United States average while in some of the so-called 'independent' homelands GNP per capita is among the lowest in Africa. To a less obvious degree the contrast between modern and traditional economy is present throughout African societies, a dynamic dualism which can be bitterly divisive.

36 National economies

National economies in Africa are very small. Nigeria and South Africa alone have a GNP in excess of US$50 billion per annum. Nigeria's new won pre-eminence was lost in 1981 because of reduced oil receipts, which also affected Algeria and Libya. With Egypt, Morocco and Ivory Coast which have more diversified economies, these are the only African countries with a GNP per annum of over US$10 billion. They are the only states with a GNP large enough to place them in the list of the world's 100 largest industrial companies by annual turnover. Not one African economy is as large as the annual turnover by Exxon. The smallest of all, St Thomas and Prince Islands, had a GNP in 1981 of US$40 million. Here is the economic manifestation of political balkanization.

In thirty-eight African states the agricultural sector accounted for more than 20 per cent of GDP, and in fifteen states for more than 40 per cent. Because in most African countries the agricultural sector is very poor, to achieve such a high proportion of GDP requires extremely high proportions of workers engaged in agriculture, and Africa is very largely a continent of agriculturalists. There is a strong correlation between a high proportion of GDP derived from agriculture and overall poverty in Africa. All the poorest states derive over 40 per cent of their GDP from agriculture. They include the Sahelian states and Ethiopia and many of the very small states.

Mining, including oil and gas exploitation, accounts for more than 20 per cent of GDP in six states including Africa's three major oil producers: Nigeria, Libya and Algeria. The Libyan economy depends on petroleum production for 55 per cent of GDP. Gabon's small economy is dominated by oil and manganese, whilst iron-ore is the mainstay of the Liberian economy. South Africa's mineral riches are diverse and mining has always been at the heart of South Africa's industrialization. For much of this century the proportional contribution of mining to GDP has declined steadily as secondary and tertiary industries grew, but since the early 1970s mining's share of GDP expanded sharply, partly because of rising gold prices and partly because of a re-expansion of the mining sector reflecting the scouring of the world for raw materials by industrialized states with few natural resources of their own. In this way South Africa is perhaps returning to a more colonial-type economy and may be likened to an individual living off capital.

Manufacturing development depends very much on the size of the domestic market and the amount of tariff protection given. The most industrialized country in Africa is South Africa which has actively pursued import substitution

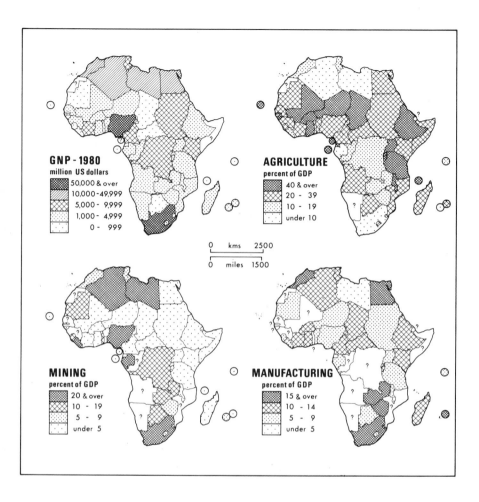

GNP - 1980
million US dollars
- 50,000 & over
- 10,000 - 49,999
- 5,000 - 9,999
- 1,000 - 4,999
- 0 - 999

AGRICULTURE
percent of GDP
- 40 & over
- 20 - 39
- 10 - 19
- under 10

0 kms 2500
0 miles 1500

MINING
percent of GDP
- 20 & over
- 10 - 19
- 5 - 9
- under 5

MANUFACTURING
percent of GDP
- 15 & over
- 10 - 14
- 5 - 9
- under 5

since 1924. Industries such as automobile production have moved steadily from assembly to incremental programmes of manufacture, with the state making key investments through its pioneering Industrial Development Corporation. Zimbabwe (as Rhodesia) and Zambia followed on the basis of much smaller markets and fewer resources. Egypt and Morocco also have relatively large manufacturing sectors. Many other African countries aspire to industrialization although the wisdom of taking that path to economic development is now seriously questioned. Import substitution industries seem almost to stimulate rather than satisfy the appetite for imports, manufacturing-led inflation often occurs and development resources are diverted from agriculture and rural areas to urban-based development with its associated problems.

117

37 Traditional economic systems

The vast majority of Africans are rural dwellers living directly off the land by different subsistence systems adapted to their physical environments. Some small groups of hunter–gatherers still survive in remote parts of Africa notably the San (Bushmen) in 'the lost world of the Kalahari', and Pygmy groups in the tropical rain-forest areas. They live by hunting animals, collecting edible fruits and roots, and sometimes tending small 'gardens' which are visited on a seasonal cycle as part of a nomadic round within a defined territory. Left adequate space by encroaching pastoralists and cultivators, hunting and gathering is a viable means of subsistence calling for an intimate and infinitely complex relationship with the physical environment.

Various forms of pastoralism dominate the drier areas of Africa. Some are nomadic, some settled and some, as in Botswana, a combination of both. All are extensive in their use of land and, in their different ways, represent complex human responses to the problems of living in difficult semi-arid environments. Nomadic pastoralists migrate with their animals in search of grazing and water. Their wanderings follow well-defined annual circuits from one known source of food to another, returning each year to a home base. The system is vulnerable to the vagaries of climate in marginal lands where rainfall is low, unreliable and subject to periodic drought.

In large parts of tropical Africa permanent cultivation is not possible because of rapid soil impoverishment once the natural vegetation cover has been removed. Shifting cultivation is a response to these environmental conditions. Plots of land are carefully selected, cleared for cultivation and the accumulated debris burnt to produce ash. The plots are then planted perhaps for two years before the cultivator moves on to a new plot, leaving the forest to regenerate and replenish the old plot. There are many forms of shifting cultivation and all are extensive in the use of land and can only be practised in areas of low population density. As the population in Africa grows, so shifting cultivation contracts.

Much sedentary agriculture in Africa incorporates an element of rotational fallow to help maintain soil fertility. Within such systems gardens near the houses are usually permanently cultivated, their fertility maintained by intensive husbandry and the application of manures and compost. In the more extensively cultivated fields a variety of crops is interplanted to ensure a balanced depletion of soil nutrients. Rotational fallow systems are based on permanent settlements and allow high densities of population.

Permanent cultivation is possible only in relatively few favoured areas in

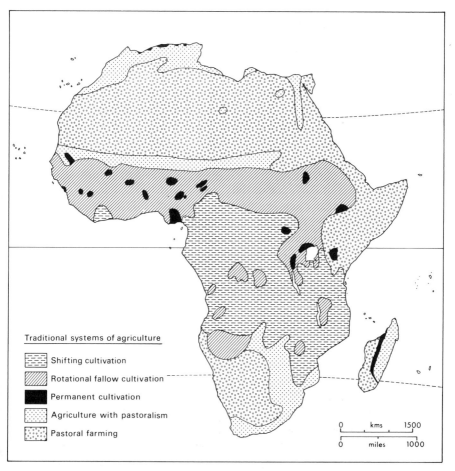

Traditional systems of agriculture

- Shifting cultivation
- Rotational fallow cultivation
- Permanent cultivation
- Agriculture with pastoralism
- Pastoral farming

```
0        kms        1500
0        miles       1000
```

Africa, on rich volcanic soils and in river valleys where fertility is renewed annually by silt deposits during seasonal floods. In areas such as Buganda it is possible to grow perennial crops, plantains and bananas, which replenish soil fertility in a natural cycle. Permanent cultivation usually supports very high densities of population.

Traditional economic systems are under great pressure throughout Africa. Balances between man and environment have been upset directly and indirectly, often in the cause of progress elsewhere. The dam that prevents flooding also prevents soil renewal, the wage-earner enticed to the mines is one less hand in the fields, the infant's life saved is one more mouth to feed. As yet too little effort has been made to help the traditional economies in Africa accommodate necessary change.

38 Cash crops

Cash crops, as the name implies, are grown to be sold, in the African context usually on export markets to earn foreign exchange. They are the mainstay of many African economies, and in some states are the only exports. They form a part of a system of agriculture and commodity trading, devised largely during the colonial period. The crops grown are mainly tropical, and are sold to the metropolitan countries which controlled the colonial empires in Africa providing them with a range of exotic commodities and enabling the colonies to pay their way. To help guarantee supplies the system of tropical plantation agriculture grew up. In territories where physical conditions were suitable land was taken up and planted with crops, usually on the basis of monoculture. For some crops, such as rubber, considerable investment was called for, not just in clearing the land and planting, but also in waiting for the trees to mature. Terrible mistakes were made by selecting the wrong place, or underestimating the task of clearing the land, or because of disease. Perhaps the most spectacular failure was the 'groundnuts affair' in post-war Tanganyika where the British colonial office, in an apparently attractive project, among other things tried to use ex-Second World War Sherman tanks to clear and deracinate vast areas around Dodoma, which turned out to be totally unsuited for groundnut monoculture. But generally the system worked and when independence came it was maintained as newly independent countries thirsted after foreign exchange to help fund economic development. It is only in recent years that the full implications of implanting this system of agriculture have been fully scrutinized, especially as countries dependent on cash crops have found that the terms of trade have moved consistently against them, making cash crops a far less attractive prospect than they once seemed.

Plantation agriculture required, in addition to the financial investment, technical and managerial skills from the metropolitan country and two important local commodities, land and labour. Almost invariably land given over to cash crops was land alienated from traditional occupance. Not only did that cause trouble at the time of alienation and disrupted traditional agriculture but, as populations grew in the colonial and post-colonial period, it was a root cause of land shortage. This is particularly acute in some countries, notably Kenya and Zimbabwe, where a great deal of land was alienated, much of it for cash crops in one form or other. Peasants were forced to enter the money economy through the device of imposing a hut or poll tax, to provide labour for the plantations which so helped deplete the labour available to the traditional sector, without a

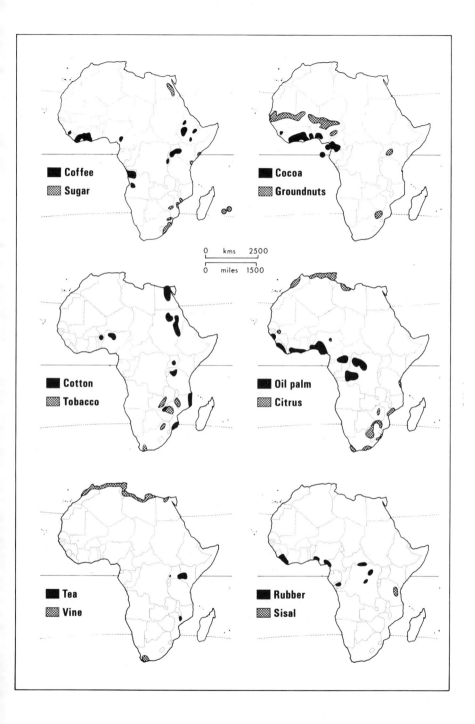

Coffee
Sugar

Cocoa
Groundnuts

0   kms   2500
0   miles   1500

Cotton
Tobacco

Oil palm
Citrus

Tea
Vine

Rubber
Sisal

compensatory input. To make matters worse the plantations took only the best workers, the young and healthy.

Plantation monoculture is peculiarly vulnerable to technical problems including disease and adverse weather conditions, and also to economic problems such as product substitution and price fluctuation. Monoculture is often extended to whole countries which are almost totally dependent on a single cash crop commodity for all their foreign exchange earnings. The prosperity of Mauritius and Reunion depend almost entirely on sugar, a commodity subject to overproduction and therefore low prices, not least because many European countries have become self-sufficient through growing beet-sugar. Senegal and Gambia are both heavily dependent on groundnuts exported whole, shelled, or as oil or cake. Sudan, Egypt, Mali and Chad are largely dependent on cotton, another commodity which has suffered from competition from substitutes in the form of man-made fibres. Commodity prices are subject to sharp fluctuations because of a host of factors ranging from crop failures in one part of the world to stockpiling in another. To take the uncertainty away attempts are made under the auspices of UN agencies like the United Nations Conference on Trade and Development (UNCTAD) to set up international commodity agreements which guarantee basic prices and impose production quotas. These do not extend to all commodities and do not always work. In overall terms commodity prices have fallen relative to prices of manufactured goods and African countries dependent on cash crops have suffered accordingly. The main problem is probably overproduction of various commodities grown under a system which is well dispersed throughout the former colonial empires of the world.

The cash crop sector while earning foreign exchange through its exports also uses much of it up because it uses a relatively high level of technology which has to be imported leaving less to be used elsewhere in the economy, perhaps to fund diversification. The possibilities of doing more processing of commodities in the producing countries are limited not least because of resistance from the industrialized consumer countries.

In some African countries, while still dependent on cash crops, there has been a move away from the plantation system. Peasant farmers have been encouraged to grow cash crops interplanted with their subsistence crops. To do this successfully it is necessary to have an efficient growers' co-operative and marketing board type of system offering guaranteed prices, making seed available, providing technical assistance and ensuring that crops are efficiently collected, graded and exported. All this is costly to organize and cannot easily be achieved when international prices fluctuate widely. The whole cash crop industry is fraught with difficulty but it is a system in which many African countries are very deeply involved and out of which there is no easy way.

Cash crop production, 1983 (1000 tonnes)

Cash crop	World	Africa (%)	Leading African producers	
Cashew nuts	467	164 (35.1)	Mozambique	70
			Nigeria	36
			Tanzania	35
Cocoa	1,557	865 (55.6)	Ivory Coast	400
			Ghana	160
			Nigeria	150
Coffee	5,537	1,188 (21.5)	Ivory Coast	225
			Ethiopia	204
			Uganda	192
Cotton lint	14,692	1,203 (8.2)	Egypt	410
			Sudan	210
			Ivory Coast	66
Groundnuts (in shell)	19,792	4,099 (20.7)	Sudan	900
			Senegal	650
			Nigeria	450
Palm oil	5,870	1,351 (23.0)	Nigeria	710
			Zaire	140
			Ivory Coast	133
Pineapples	8,665	1,257 (14.5)	Ivory Coast	350
			South Africa	237
			Kenya	160
Rubber	3,866	180 (4.7)	Liberia	65
			Nigeria	40
			Ivory Coast	27
Sisal	384	179 (46.6)	Tanzania	82
			Kenya	51
			Angola	20
Sugar cane	888,735	63,483 (7.1)	South Africa	13,370
			Egypt	9,000
			Mauritius	5,500
Tea	2,020	223 (11.0)	Kenya	112
			Malawi	38
			Tanzania	18
Tobacco	6,090	318 (5.2)	Zimbabwe	98
			Malawi	72
			South Africa	38
Wines	33,388	1,100 (3.3)	South Africa	660
			Algeria	264
			Morocco	83

Source: FAO Production Annual, 1983.

39 Ghana and Ivory Coast

Not only has our [cocoa] production level fallen by almost half, but the price our cocoa commands has fallen to one-third of its average price five years ago. These are the harsh realities of our situation.

(Flt Lt Jerry Rawlings of Ghana, *West Africa*, 3 January 1983)

Receipts from the export of cocoa and coffee have fallen from 900,000m. CFA francs to 225,000m in three years and the state is stocking 175,000 tonnes of coffee in its silos.

(Felix Houphouët-Boigny of Ivory Coast, *West Africa* 14 February 1983)

Thus the shared predicament of two neighbouring West African states whose economies depend very largely on cash crop commodity exports is summed up. The statements also give clues to important differences between the two states.

Having set the political pace to independence in black Africa Ghana also tried to break the economic mould of dependence on cash crop exports. Kwame Nkrumah used a healthy economic base, built on cash crops, for centrally planned development aimed at industrialization. Roads were built, the new port of Tema constructed and, on the Volta river, the Akosombo hydroelectric dam was commissioned. The dam was part of an integrated plan for mining Ghanaian bauxite and using the cheap electricity for an alumina plant and a smelter. Nkrumah was forced to settle for the dam and the smelter which was fed imported alumina from the West Indies. The plans were over-ambitious, infrastructural investment could not yield immediate returns and money was wasted on prestige projects. Ghana's economy became overstretched and in 1966 Nkrumah was overthrown. For all his vision, ability and drive Nkrumah had been unable to beat the system. Ghana moved through a succession of governments, the economy went from bad to worse and many Ghanaians gravitated to Nigeria as oil boomed there in the 1970s.

Ivory Coast followed different political and economic paths. Houphouët-Boigny has been in power since independence and has deliberately made Ivory Coast a client state of France. About 45,000 French are resident in Ivory Coast working in the civil service and the professions. With French help a series of development plans were drawn up giving priority to the cash crop sector led by coffee, cocoa and palm oil. They were successfully implemented, targets were reached, exports flourished and the 'economic miracle' of the Ivory Coast became a reality. It brought with it a hydroelectricity dam at Kossou and a new

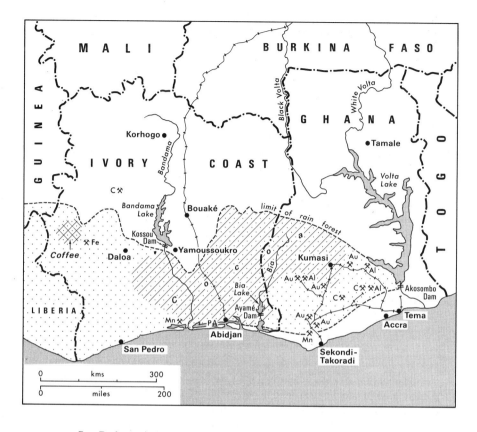

port at San Pedro to help spread development away from Abidjan. As steadily as Ghana fell down the GDP per capita league table so Ivory Coast rose. Conservative leadership, political stability and, sadly, neo-colonialism, were seen to pay.

Recently Ivory Coast and Ghana have been hit by plummeting commodity prices. In Ghana the response was a succession of different governments. In Ivory Coast they discovered oil in quantities large enough for self-sufficiency in 1983 – who does not believe in miracles? Ghana has also been hit by the enforced exodus from Nigeria. Perhaps Jerry Rawlings can turn it to advantage, work his own miracle and use the influx to regenerate Ghana's rural sector and build slowly from there. It is a long shot especially as the bright lights of Lagos are already beckoning again.

40 Minerals and mining

Africa is extremely rich in minerals and mining is one of the few available means of accelerating economic growth. The richest states in Africa are all dependent for their prosperity on mineral exploitation and many others in Africa would like to emulate them. But there are serious drawbacks: mining is an exhaustive activity, demand fluctuates and with it prices. Because minerals are mainly exported as raw materials most of the benefit goes to others. For a mineral-dependent country it is at best a race to use the wealth generated by mining to modernize the traditional economy and put it on a sound footing before the minerals run out. At worst it is a once-and-for-all bonanza followed by economic disaster.

Africa's share of world mineral resources is impressive: two-thirds or more of the world's production of gold, diamonds and cobalt; 40 per cent or more of the world's platinum, chrome and manganese; 10 per cent or more of phosphates, uranium, copper, bauxite and iron-ore. By value the most important mineral in Africa in recent years has been petroleum. In 1980 Africa accounted for 9.5 per cent of world production but the oil slump saw that share fall to 7.9 per cent in 1981. Nigeria, Libya, Algeria and Egypt each produced more than 1 per cent of world output in 1981 and together more than 87 per cent of Africa's oil. Gabon, Angola, Congo and Tunisia are among Africa's other oil producers who are also exporters on a scale which significantly affects their own economies.

Petroleum apart, the greatest concentration of mineral wealth is in southern Africa, the world's largest single source of gold, diamonds, cobalt, platinum, chrome and copper. South African gold comes from an arc of reefs 300 miles (480 km) long in the southern Transvaal and Orange Free State. In 1981 South Africa exported 644 tons of gold valued at R8,557 million. Zaire is the largest producer of industrial diamonds from Kasai province but Namibia has the greatest resource of gemstones on the sea beaches of the Namib desert coast north of the Orange river mouth and in marine deposits immediately off-shore. There are many diamond pipes in South Africa, and in Botswana two pipes, Orapa and Lethlakana, were opened in the 1970s. Platinum group metals are found in the Bushveld Complex around Rustenburg north-west of Johannesburg in the Transvaal. These deposits are the richest in the world and contain a very high proportion of world reserves and are the only major source outside the Soviet Union. Chrome, another rare metal, is also associated with the South African Bushveld Complex and is also found in Zimbabwe. The copperbelt of central Africa which is bisected by the Zaire–Zambia boundary accounts for over

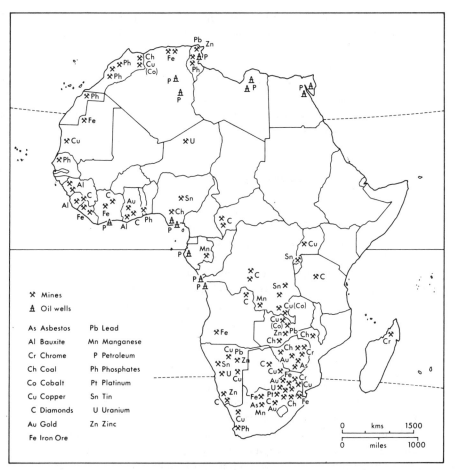

75 per cent of Africa's copper production. In Zaire it is closely associated with cobalt, another rare and strategically important mineral. South African copper mining is mainly of low-grade ore at Phalaborwa in the eastern Transvaal. In Botswana at Selibe-Pikwe, operational since 1974, the copper is associated with nickel. In the mid-1970s South Africa invested R600 million in the ultimate integrated mining and transportation operation. Production of high-grade (67 per cent) iron-ore from deposits of 4000 million tons around Sishen in the northern Cape province was expanded to over 30 million tons per annum. To handle the iron-ore, and that alone, a 538 mile (861 km) railway was built to Saldanha Bay where a new deep-water port capable of handling 250,000 dwt ore-carriers was constructed. Minerals in southern Africa are big business and come in big projects.

The coastal states of west and north Africa also have considerable mineral deposits other than oil. In Liberia and Mauritania the smaller forerunners of Sishen–Saldanha Bay are to be found: Nimba–Buchanan, Bomi Hills–Monrovia and Zouerate–Nouadhibou while in Sierra Leone similar railways have already been ripped up as the iron-ore has been exhausted. Bu Craa–El Aaiun in Western Sahara provides a variation on the theme, for phosphates are carried on a trunk conveyor belt. Vast areas of Africa have not yet been adequately surveyed or prospected and many major mineral resources await discovery.

Modern mining in Africa is large scale and surviving examples of small alluvial workings such as for diamonds in Sierra Leone and Lesotho are very few. Mining is usually in the hands of large multinational corporations even where African states have adopted some form of nationalization for their mining sector. These companies have the finance, information, technical know-how, managerial skills and marketing contacts to carry out the mining enterprise most efficiently. In dealing with such companies the individual state is almost invariably at a disadvantage and as a result the proceeds from mining accruing to the state are limited. The companies originated in the industrialized countries and are part of a world trading system that works very much to the advantage of those countries. African minerals, exported as raw materials, are turned into manufactured goods in the industrialized countries. The long-term trend is for raw material prices to fall relative to prices of manufactured goods. The African country dependent on mineral exports generally sees a substantial share of the proceeds from mining go to the foreign mining company usually for investment elsewhere, then has to suffer falling relative prices for its raw material exports and rising relative prices for its manufactured imports.

The mining enterprise is often isolated from the rest of the economy as if it were an enclave. It is often so capital-intensive as to require very little labour and the massive, fiendishly expensive equipment has to be imported. An open-cast diamond mine such as Orapa functions with a minimal production work-force. Each shift a bulldozer, loader and some 40-ton trucks need to be driven but very little else in actual mining. There are of course, process workers, surveyors and managers and the service workers needed to keep the plant and machinery operative as well as to meet the needs of a small mining township isolated on the Kalahari fringe. The iron-ore railways of west Africa bring little benefit to the people living between mine and port, and when the mine goes the railway goes too.

On the other hand the enclave economy concept can mislead because there is a disruptive drain of young men from the traditional economy to the mines, often induced by rural taxation. This is nowhere better illustrated than in South Africa where the 'homelands' have been run down partly as a consequence of the pernicious migrant labour system devised to meet the labour requirements of the mines. Such a dual economy which is found in many parts of Africa comprises two dynamic elements, one feeding off the other.

The rate of mineral extraction is usually controlled by the mining company. The extreme example is in diamonds where De Beers have cornered the world market including the marketing of the Soviet Union's production. Many African leaders are acutely aware that their meagre prosperity depends on a wasting asset but cannot afford to do without these proceeds from selling as quickly or as slowly as the companies dictate. In January 1983 President Bongo embarrassed President Mitterrand on his visit to Gabon by asking France to provide Gabon with a nuclear power station 'for when the oil runs out'. It will be interesting to see how industrialized countries respond to such pleas which are backed by the argument 'you have enjoyed the benefits of using up our finite resources, now you help us'.

Gabon is a state which has benefited greatly from mineral exploitation. The combination of a small population and moderate resources of oil and manganese have placed it second only to Libya in the GDP per capita league table ever since independence. Libya is a one-resource state based on oil. South Africa derives much of its wealth, and an increasing share of its GDP, from minerals. The Nigerian economy, the largest in Africa, is underpinned by oil. Riches in Africa are usually mineral riches. Botswana was one of the poorer states in Africa in terms of GDP per capita until the 1970s. Then on the basis of diamond-mining (begun in 1971) and copper and nickel (1974) Botswana began to climb steadily up the league table to seventeenth in 1975 and tenth in 1980.

Some African countries are almost totally dependent on minerals. Zambia is the extreme example with 97 per cent of exports copper, but in Algeria, Gabon, Guinea, Libya, Mauritania and Nigeria minerals account for more than 90 per cent of exports and most are dependent on just one mineral. Such economies are vulnerable in the long term to resource exhaustion. In the short term they are vulnerable to price fluctuation beyond their control. The effect of the world oil glut on Nigeria's economy illustrates the point writ large. Producers' cartels such as OPEC have limited power to regulate prices in the long run. Dependence goes much deeper; a dependent economy is usually associated with dependent political and social structures and many African states are in this condition.

41 One Zambia, one nation

'Let us go forward together and build one Zambia, one nation.' So President Kaunda urges his people to face the task of nation-building. The task is daunting, to forge national unity among 5 million people of seventy-two ethno-linguistic groups lumped together by the logic of a grotesque colonial boundary. Zambia is economically dependent on a single resource, copper; it is land-locked, and since independence has been on the colonial front-line in Africa, exposed to the hostility of white minority regimes to the south.

At independence copper dominated the Zambian economy, contributing, in round figures, 95 per cent of exports, 60 per cent of government revenue and 15 per cent of paid employment. These figures have not changed significantly in twenty years. The overwhelming dominance of copper leads to serious social and geographical concentrations of wealth. More importantly the terms of trade have overall moved against Zambia as the price of copper has fallen steeply relative to the price of imported manufactures.

Government policies have been aimed at economic diversification, social redistribution of wealth and regional development. Emphasis has been given to rural development and the improvement of peasant agriculture in which the vast majority is engaged. Industrial development has been stimulated by direct government investment, the provision of adequate infrastructure and by the erection of tariff walls. Regional development has been a feature of Zambia's national plans, effected by improving accessibility and directing industrial location. Not all Zambians back such policies and the government has frequently been locked into conflict with copper mine-workers organized as a powerful industrial élite. Import substitution policies have been inflationary and production targets have not been reached. A strong axis of development has emerged southwards from the copperbelt, through Kabwe and Lusaka to Kafue and Kariba. It neatly bisects Zambia leaving vast wings of underdevelopment on both sides. There have been errors and inefficiencies but their effect pales alongside the worsening terms of trade and having had to take the brunt of the Rhodesian conflict.

Zambia's vulnerability as a land-locked state was underscored when, following the Rhodesian unilateral declaration of independence (UDI), the effect of the oil embargo against Rhodesia was only to prevent oil reaching Zambia. In 1968 an oil pipeline was built from Dar es Salaam but Zambia's vital copper exports remained vulnerable. Western agencies, insistent on financial criteria, were unwilling to build a railway from Dar es Salaam. The Chinese had

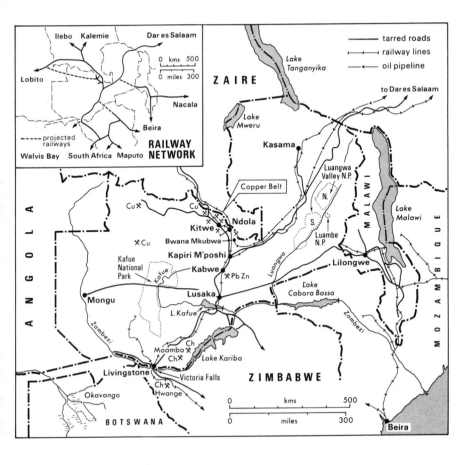

no such inhibitions and constructed the Tazara railway by 1975. Port congestion and low-carrying capacity on the political railway have limited its usefulness and it is a drain on Zambia's meagre resources.

The whole of Zambia's existence has been a struggle against dependence on the south, a political history of defiant policies and projects on the heroic scale punctuated by an economic history of humiliating defeats as dependence is re-enforced through maize shortages, railway inefficiencies and route blockages. Peripheral to South Africa's economic core, Zambia has tried without lasting success to escape from its orbital path. In late 1982 Zambia became the first African state to have to 'reschedule' its outstanding loan and interest repayments, a small episode in the world banking crisis but traumatic for an emergent nation against whom all the economic cards have been stacked since independence.

42 Regional economic groupings

The burden of Kwame Nkrumah's message, 'Africa must unite', applies as much, if not more, to the economic as to the political sphere. The political balkanization of Africa resulted in the creation of large numbers of small, weak, economically dependent national units. In these circumstances many African countries have come together in attempts to overcome the economic problems of scale. There have been failures but some groups are now making encouraging progress.

The East African Community based on common services built up in the colonial period fell apart in the late 1970s. Regional economic imbalances favoured Kenya but no adequate means of compensation was found for Tanzania and Uganda. Important ideological frictions arose between Kenya and Tanzania, and Idi Amin provided a different *coup de grâce*.

French colonial groupings tended to survive because independence came simultaneously to all territories and many of them needed economic support. *L'Union Douaniere et Economique de L'Afrique Centrale* (UDEAC) succeeded AEF as a customs union in 1966 and also aimed to promote economic development. It is less ambitious and its services less centralized than at first conceived but it has survived. *Organization Commune Africaine et Mauricienne* (OCAM), another Francophone group, has had many defections and now concentrates on technical and cultural co-operation. *Communauté Economique de L'Afrique de l'Ouest* (CEAO), the successor to AOF, aims to lower customs duties between members and promote economic development, aims shared by ECOWAS to which all the CEAO states belong. As a result CEAO could disappear or possibly change its emphasis.

ECOWAS, formed in 1975, groups sixteen west African states from different colonial backgrounds. It aims to liberalize trade towards customs union and to promote regional co-operation through commissions for agriculture, industry, energy, trade, transport and telecommunications. Advances have been made but there are problems. The aim of free movement of peoples suffered a serious set-back when Nigeria expelled foreign workers in early 1983, although it was soon reported that Ghanaians were returning to Lagos with ECOWAS documents. The future of ECOWAS depends very much on Nigeria, its largest member with half its population and one-third of aggregate GDP.

The rival ideologies of SADCC and South Africa are diametrically opposed over economic development in southern Africa and the *verligte* Southern African

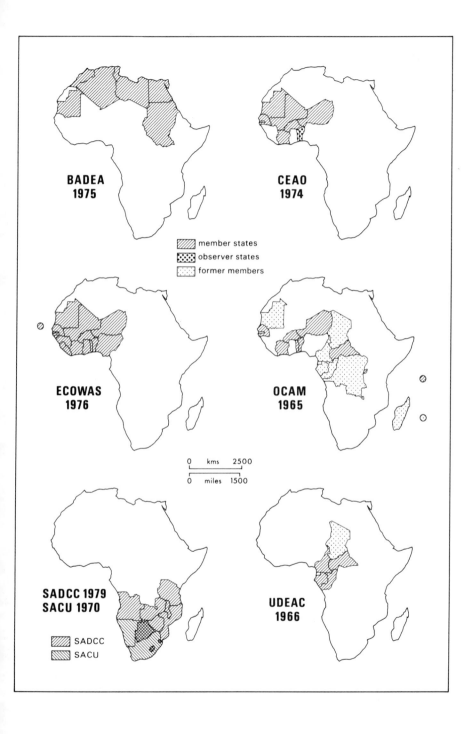

BADEA
1975

CEAO
1974

member states
observer states
former members

ECOWAS
1976

OCAM
1965

0   kms   2500

0   miles   1500

SADCC 1979
SACU 1970

SADCC
SACU

UDEAC
1966

Customs Union (SACU) aimed to keep the former High Commission Territories snugly under South Africa's wing. The Arab Bank for Economic Development in Africa (BADEA) grew from an attempt by Arab League oil producers to offset the worst effects of high oil prices on the poorer countries of Africa into a development aid agency open to all members of the OAU.

43 Mano River Union

The Mano river forms part of the boundary between the two small Guinea Coast republics of Liberia and Sierra Leone. On 3 October 1973 its name was given to a union between the two countries aimed at improving economic development and integration. In October 1980 the neighbouring Republic of Guinea joined the union in an important extension of this experiment in economic co-operation.

Liberia and Sierra Leone have similar origins as coastal settlements for freed slaves respectively under American and British protection. All three countries have very similar economies. The greater part of the population is engaged in agriculture, some of which is cash crop, but all three are heavily dependent on minerals exported as raw materials. In Liberia the main minerals are iron-ore and diamonds which account for about 80 per cent of exports; in Guinea bauxite makes up over 90 per cent of exports; and in Sierra Leone diamonds and bauxite account for over 50 per cent. The vulnerability of a state dependent on minerals is nowhere better illustrated than in Sierra Leone where, after forty years of operation, iron-ore mining ceased abruptly in 1975 leaving thousands unemployed and, in the words of President Siaka Stevens, 'with not a token of development in the whole of the [mining] areas'. Even the railways which had served the iron-ore mines were ripped up. To add to Sierra Leone's plight diamond production fell steadily from 921,904 carats in 1971 to 176,143 carats in 1981 while smuggling increased and prices fell. Worse still, mining development had 'undermined' the agricultural sector not least because diamonds in Sierra Leone are found in alluvial deposits and thousands 'try their luck' legally and illegally. Once a net exporter of its staple diet, rice, Sierra Leone now has to import virtually all. The mineral failure not surprisingly led to a major economic crisis and the only way out is more of the same, underground mining of a Kimberlite diamond pipe!

In all three states identified mineral resources are made accessible from the coast by railways used exclusively for minerals. The railways are of different gauges, 4 ft 8.5 in (1.435 m) and 3 ft 6 in (1.065 m) in Liberia and 3 ft 3 in (1 m) and 4 ft 8.5 in (1.435 m) in Guinea, while the former railways in Sierra Leone were 2 ft 6 in (0.765 m), clearly showing that there was never any intention of lateral linkages. One of the aims of the Mano River Union (MRU) is precisely that, the construction of a lateral transport link, the US$97 million Freetown–Monrovia highway, work on which was due to begin in 1983.

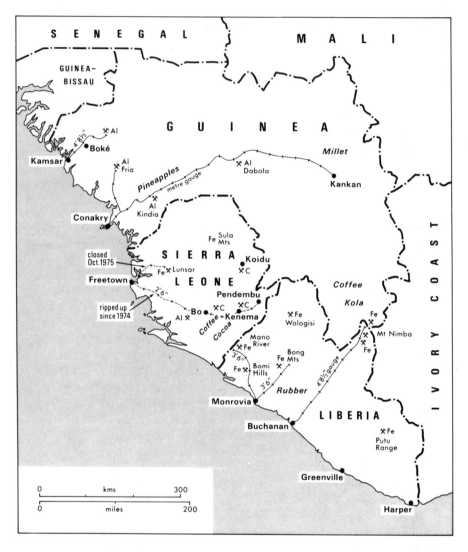

The MRU is also hoping to attract funds for the Mano River Basin Development Project centred on a hydroelectricity scheme. Co-operation in agriculture and industry is being planned with the long-term aim of establishing a customs union. These are small beginnings in a group of poor, dependent countries with similar economic characteristics. The scope for development based on complementarity is obviously minute but in the MRU no one state is dominant and their coming together might make it easier to attract development funds. Like CEAO the MRU is totally contained within ECOWAS which has similar aims on a much wider scale. In 1982 ECOWAS agreed to study the relationship between itself and the two smaller bodies contained within it. The difference in scale and emphasis probably gives scope for the MRU to remain active within ECOWAS without any serious incompatibility.

44 Energy resources and utilization

Africa is well endowed with energy resources and vast areas not yet prospected in detail will yield much more. Africa actually produces three times the amount of energy consumed on the continent. Yet several African states had their economies crippled by upward spiralling energy prices in the 1970s. The distribution of energy resources is far from even and the few states with a large surplus of energy production over consumption sell their produce on world markets at prices the poor countries of Africa can ill afford.

In 1980 Africa produced 619 million tonnes of coal equivalent and consumed 186 million tonnes. Yet only twelve African states produced more energy than they consumed; forty-one were net importers of energy. The imbalance of energy production and consumption was such that Libya, Nigeria, Gabon, Congo and Angola all produced more than ten times the energy they used. In 1981 Africa produced 229 million tonnes of oil and consumed 76 million tonnes. Oil production came from twelve countries, nine of which were net exporters. Nigeria, Libya, Algeria and Egypt together account for 87 per cent of output. South Africa produced 95 per cent of African coal: 127 million tonnes in 1981. To make up for its lack of oil South Africa converts low-grade coal to oil; in 1981 the two Sasol plants in production used 13.2 million tonnes of coal for this purpose. Low pithead prices enable South African coal to compete on world markets despite high transport costs and in 1981 30 million tonnes were exported. Other coal producers in Africa are Zimbabwe, Zambia, Morocco and Mozambique. Hydroelectricity in Africa comes largely from large dams such as Aswan, Akosombo, Kariba, Cabora Bassa and Owen Falls. The output from several of them is in excess of local consumption and electricity is sold to neighbouring states. Virtually all the uranium produced in Africa, in South Africa, Namibia and Niger, is exported. Only South Africa has a nuclear power station.

Oil often distinguishes rich from poor in Africa. Algeria, Libya, Gabon, Congo and Angola, the only African states with a favourable balance of trade, are all oil exporters. The trade deficit of most other states is largely due to the high cost of oil imports. The poverty of the Sahelian and Horn States is confirmed by energy patterns: they consume little but produce less. Energy resources and utilization confirm and partly explain patterns of wealth and poverty in Africa noted elsewhere.

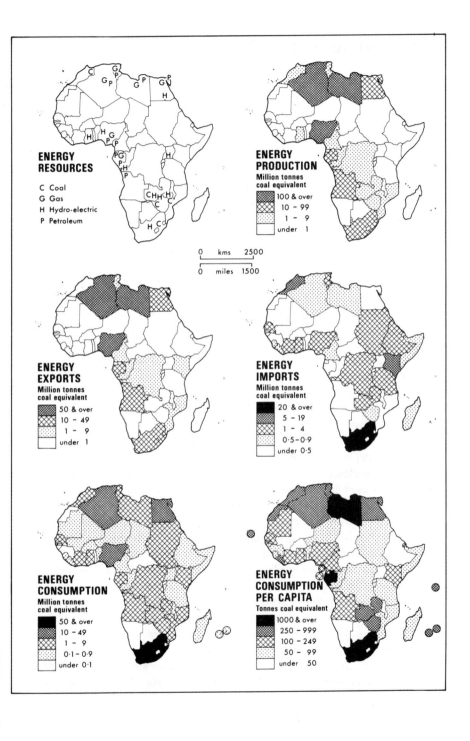

ENERGY RESOURCES

C Coal
G Gas
H Hydro-electric
P Petroleum

ENERGY PRODUCTION
Million tonnes
coal equivalent

- 100 & over
- 10 – 99
- 1 – 9
- under 1

ENERGY EXPORTS
Million tonnes
coal equivalent

- 50 & over
- 10 – 49
- 1 – 9
- under 1

ENERGY IMPORTS
Million tonnes
coal equivalent

- 20 & over
- 5 – 19
- 1 – 4
- 0·5 – 0·9
- under 0·5

ENERGY CONSUMPTION
Million tonnes
coal equivalent

- 50 & over
- 10 – 49
- 1 – 9
- 0·1 – 0·9
- under 0·1

ENERGY CONSUMPTION PER CAPITA
Tonnes coal equivalent

- 1000 & over
- 250 – 999
- 100 – 249
- 50 – 99
- under 50

0   kms   2500

0   miles   1500

45 Harnessing Africa's rivers

Water is the critical resource of Africa. Large areas of the continent are deficient in water to the extent that cultivation is impossible. Other areas have a marked excess of water, often seasonal, leading to waste of a scarce resource and to destruction of land and life: drought and flood are characteristic of much of Africa. Yet irrigation and hydroelectric potential is very high. Therefore there is a premium on controlling and harnessing Africa's rivers.

Irrigation is most effective in those areas of Africa lying between the high rainfall equatorial zone and the deserts, an 'irrigation belt' from Senegal, through the Sahel, the Sudan, the Horn and east Africa, and most of southern Africa. Over this vast area low rainfall and high evapotranspiration conspire so that cultivation is made possible or at least is greatly improved by irrigation. Availability of water is critical: some small schemes use pumped groundwater but the overwhelming majority of irrigation projects use water from rivers and lakes. The largest schemes are to be found where great rivers such as the Nile, Niger and Orange cross the irrigation belt.

The high plateau surfaces of Africa, often saucer-like in structure, present an escarpment to the sea. Over and through this escarpment the rivers of Africa plunge, their volume and head of fall providing the continent with the world's greatest potential in hydroelectric power, much of it in the great river valleys which also have high irrigation potential.

Most African rivers have a seasonably variable regime. River courses are often completely dry in one season, full of raging torrents in another. River mouths are sand-dune blocked lagoons for most of the year but then, in flash floods, spew out vast quantities of liquefied top-soil to discolour the sea for miles from the shore. River flow is erratic, river flood is devastating. Protection can come only from careful control, an integrated system which involves not just the massive concrete structures of Aswan and Kariba but also the small earth dams on minor streams and headwaters. Some idea of the scale of the enterprise of river control needed in Africa may be gained from the fact that in South Africa alone there are already more than half a million dams of all sizes. The process of controlling Africa's rivers has a long way to go.

Many large dams have been built in post-independence Africa. Most were primarily to produce cheap electricity, but some were also for irrigation and other purposes. Dams are beloved of politicians, national plan-makers, financiers and aid-donors alike. They are potent symbols of economic virility and political prestige; they are clearly visible, concrete (!) and finite projects,

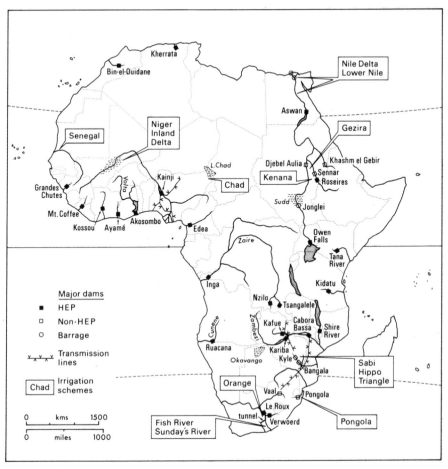

demonstrably a basis for future economic and social development.

Not surprisingly decisions to build dams often have been highly political and controversial. The Kariba dam was a symbol of federation between the Rhodesias because it straddled the boundary between them and so the technically superior Kafue site, nearer the copperbelt consumers, was passed over. Cabora Bassa, built in Portuguese Mozambique, was a manifestation of South Africa's outward-looking foreign policy. Completion of the project coincided with the independence of Mozambique, but electricity has flowed along the transmission lines to Pretoria with few interruptions. Kwame Nkrumah was not so fortunate in Ghana as he was overthrown in the year his great Akosombo dam was completed. The then high cost of the dam helped precipitate his fall. Although many African dams have been one-off projects an encouraging number are the basis for international co-operation. Akosombo electricity is supplied to Togo and Benin, and Kariba supplies both Zambia and Zimbabwe. Yet the only river basins to have been harnessed on anything approaching a fully co-ordinated system are the Nile and the Orange.

For thousands of years man has understood the character of the Nile and used it to create a great civilization based on intensive cultivation in an area surrounded by desert. Today, from the Owen Falls dam near Lake Victoria to the delta, people have sought to control and harness the Nile through modern technology. The first modern dam on the Nile was completed at Aswan in 1902 to store water for additional irrigation in the lower Nile valley and delta. It was designed to help control the Nile's flood which saw the September discharge of the river at about ten times the volume of the April discharge.

The flood comes mainly from the Ethiopian highlands via the Blue Nile which has an annual discharge about twice that of the White Nile. In 1925 the Sennar dam on the Blue Nile was completed to control that flood and to start the Gezira irrigation scheme, the largest in Africa, on the tongue of land between the two Niles south of their confluence. The first water agreement between Egypt and the Sudan in 1929 gave 5 per cent of the Nile's water to the Sudan. A new agreement in 1959 adjusted the Sudan's share to 20 per cent following a major expansion of the Gezira scheme, the Managil extension, opened in 1958. Meanwhile a further measure of flood control and water conservation was achieved by the construction of the Djebel Aulia dam on the White Nile, 30 miles (48 km) above Khartoum. This dam was to pond back the more regular flow of the White Nile when the Blue Nile was in flood, so flattening out the flood peak to give Egypt the opportunity to conserve more water at Aswan.

Such international co-operation was largely a benefit of almost all the Nile valley being under British influence, if not direct colonial control. It enabled a detailed plan for water conservation and control, irrigation and hydroelectric power to be drawn up for the whole of the Nile basin and laid the basis for the co-operation and co-ordination which has characterized water development in the Nile valley in recent years.

In 1959 the Owen Falls hydroelectric dam near the Nile's exit from Lake Victoria was completed to provide cheap electricity for economic development in Uganda and also Kenya. The Aswan High Dam, built in the 1960s 4 miles (6 km) above the first Aswan dam was both controversial and symbolic. Doubts were expressed at the wisdom of creating the world's second largest man-made lake in one of the hottest places on earth, at a site where the shallowness of the lake would add to the ratio of evaporation to storage capacity. Other experts confidently forecast that the dam would silt up very rapidly. But the real controversy, and perhaps the source of at least some of the technical doubts, was its cost, over £400 million, and the source of funding. In the political climate of

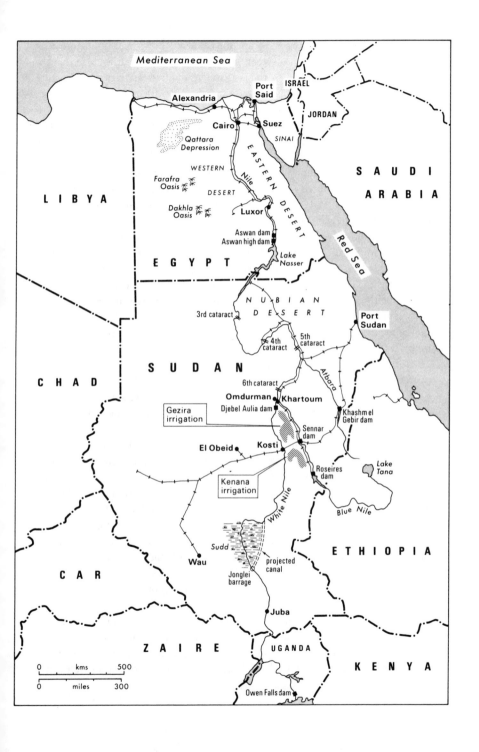

the Suez crisis of 1956 the west abruptly turned down the opportunity of financing and building the project, anticipating Nasser's fall rather than that the Russians would step in. Not for the last time in modern Africa was the west to misunderstand the motivation and determination of African leaders, and fail to appreciate the political significance of a project which, assessed in narrow economic terms, might not appear to be a viable proposition. The High Dam became as symbolic of Egypt's revolution and independence as Egypt's control of the Suez canal itself. Aswan became the gateway for the Soviet Union's entry into African affairs, though it remains their only venture of that kind in Africa. The Aswan High Dam was completed ahead of schedule to become the linchpin of the Egyptian economy. It has permitted a 20 per cent more intensive use of previously irrigated land and has allowed 5–10 per cent more land to be brought under irrigation. It provides more than half Egypt's electricity and protects the country from flood. Evaporation loss is high, about 10 per cent of annual flow, but silting is less serious than anticipated. Salinity has not been a major problem in the irrigated lands but imports of fertilizer have increased. Erosion of the delta coast is being experienced with the attendant dangers of sea-water pollution but, on balance, the project has been an outstanding success both politically and economically, so much so that it has even been suggested that Egypt now has too much water.

An interesting offshoot of the High Dam project which underlines the co-operation between Egypt and the Sudan is the new dam and irrigation scheme at Khasm el Girba on the Atbara tributary of the Nile in the eastern Sudan. Here, people displaced by the creation of Lake Nasser from the Sudanese area around Wadi Halfa have been resettled around New Halfa at a cost of £15 million borne by Egypt. At Roseiries a new dam was built across the Blue Nile in 1968 to provide additional water storage, flood control and a hydroelectric capacity. It also enabled the creation of the Kenana irrigation scheme of about 1 million acres (400,000 ha). Originally planned for commercial cotton production, the irrigation schemes are the economic heartland of the Sudan and are now also producing groundnuts and wheat as well as subsistence crops for the farmers themselves. In addition to the dams and barrages the Nile is also harnessed to many pump irrigation schemes, the possibilities for which have increased where water levels have been raised by the dams. The intensive use of existing Nile water has led to the seeking of ways to enhance the supply by conservation. The most spectacular project is a barrage at Jonglei and a 150 mile (240 km) canal to channel the water away from the Sudd to reduce the rate of evaporation and to increase the flow of the White Nile. Much remains to be done before even the Nile is fully harnessed, but the need for river basin planning is amply demonstrated and the benefits from co-operation and co-ordination are plain to see.

144

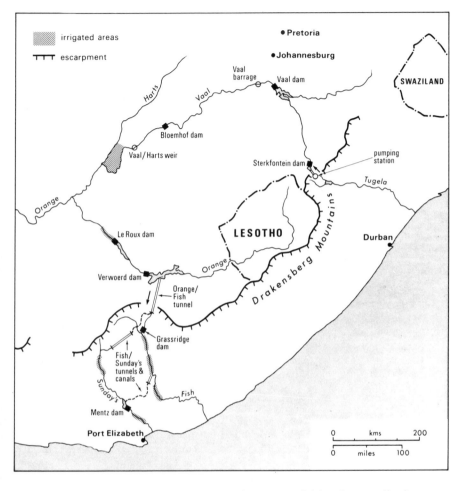

The only other African river basin whose potential has been realized to a similar degree is the Orange in South Africa. Its major tributary the Vaal, flowing westwards from the eastern plateau edge, has long been carefully conserved to provide water for Johannesburg and the Reef towns and, lower down, for the Vaal–Harts irrigation scheme. By 1974 the long-feared water supply constraint on the growth of the Witwatersrand approached as demand for Vaal water equalled reliable yield, but in the same year a project designed to augment the water yield of the Vaal came into operation. East of the Drakensberg escarpment water is in plentiful supply in the Tugela river basin, so the Tugela has been linked to the Vaal by a pumping scheme which raises Tugela water through a 1660 feet (506 m) vertical lift to the Vaal basin. There the water is stored in the new Sterkfontein earth dam in an area where evaporation is lower than at the Vaal dam which now operates at a lower capacity as a further conservation measure. The project is designed to deliver water from the Tugela to the Vaal to increase the net yield from the Vaal river system by about 25 per cent. An extension of the scheme, the Drakensberg project, involves the construction of three small dams and a 1000 MW hydroelectricity installation to supply projected demands for water in the Vaal basin to 1995.

The Orange river project also transfers large quantities of water from one river basin to another over the Great Escarpment, this time from High to Low Veld. The project, now estimated to cost about R500 million, aims to extend irrigation in the lower Orange river valley, to give a higher degree of flood control on a river where peak flow is sixteen times minimum flow, and to provide hydroelectricity as well as to transfer water from the Orange to the Fish and Sunday's river valleys below the south-eastern escarpment for irrigation purposes and for water

Selected major dams in Africa

Country	Dam	River (basin)	MW	Date
Angola	Cambambe	Cuanza	260	
Cameroon	Edea	Sanaga	270	1966
Egypt	Aswan High	Nile	2100	1970
Ghana	Akosombo	Volta	792	1966
Ivory Coast	Kossou	Bandama	180	1973
Mozambique	Cabora Bassa	Zambezi	2000	1974
Nigeria	Kainji	Niger	960	1968
South Africa	Vaal	Vaal (Orange)	—	1928
	H. F. Verwoerd	Orange	320	1971
	P. K. Le Roux	Orange	220	1977
Sudan	Sennar	Blue Nile	—	1925
	Djebel Aulia	White Nile	—	
	Roseiries	Blue Nile	—	1968
	Khasm el Gebir	Atbara (Nile)	—	
Tanzania	Kidatu	Nkulu (Rufiji)	100	1975
Uganda	Owen Falls	Victoria Nile	150	1954
Zaire	Inga I	Zaire	350	1972
	Inga II	Zaire	1000	1977
Zambia	Kafue	Kafue (Zambezi)	750	1972
	Iteshiteshi	Kafue (Zambezi)	—	1976
Zambia/Zimbabwe	Kariba	Zambezi	1600	1960

Note: Installed hydroelectric capacity (MW) shown is latest capacity which may not be the original capacity.

supply to the Port Elizabeth/Uitenhage urban-industrial complex. The H.F. Verwoerd dam across the Orange river was completed in 1971, and the P. K. Le Roux dam 90 miles (144 km) downstream in 1977. The dams have water storage capacities of about 5 million acre feet (6000 million cubic metres) and 2.5 million acre feet (3000 million cubic metres) and installed hydroelectric capacity of 320 MW and 220 MW respectively. Below the Le Roux dam it is planned eventually to irrigate some 570,000 acres (230,000 ha) in the Orange valley. In 1975 the 51 mile (82 km) in length and 16.4 feet (5 m) in diameter Orange–Fish tunnel from the Verwoerd dam to the Fish river was opened. Canals take water from there to irrigation schemes in the Fish valley and across to the lower Sunday's river valley where since 1978 Orange river water has been used to augment local water supplies to an existing irrigation scheme which had never operated at above half capacity because of water shortage.

46 Tourism

Most tourists in Africa are Europeans and the African tourist trade is geared to their demands. No more than 10 per cent of Africa's tourists come from African countries and only in southern Africa is there a major local tourist industry. The inter-continental emphasis makes tourism similar to cash crop agriculture and mining in that it mainly serves the needs of others, leaving Africans with a relatively small return.

Sunshine holidays in north Africa are long established in the European tourist trade. Sunshine, geographical proximity, cheap accommodation and above all cheap air travel make attractive economy holiday packages for literally millions of Europeans each year mainly in Morocco, Tunisia and the Canary Islands. Extension of this trade into west Africa is hampered by distance though the Gambia, Senegal and Ivory Coast have large, if not mass, tourist trades.

Elsewhere in Africa tourism depends on unique features to attract visitors over greater distances. In Egypt, the Pyramids, Sphinx, Temples and Nile itself have long brought inter-continental tourists on the grand scale as one recalls on entering the vast hotels of a bygone age in Cairo and Giza. In East Africa the unique ingredient is wildlife first glimpsed by the alert tourist as the plane approaches Nairobi airport. The East African parks are wonders of the modern world whether it be chugging up the Nile between herds of hippo to view the Kabalega Falls with the most enormous crocodiles rasping the boat's keel as they slide into the water, or in the Ngorongoro crater wondering whether that mean-looking rhino really does intend to charge your Land Rover, or finding lions high in the acacia trees in Ruwenzori and Manyara. The up-market East African package is one week in the parks and one week on the fronded Indian Ocean beaches of hot sugary coral sands.

In southern Africa the beaches and game parks also attract more affluent visitors. Kafue in Zambia, Kruger in South Africa and Etosha Pan in Namibia are all vast and teeming with wildlife. Swaziland, Lesotho and South Africa's 'independent' homelands have a thriving tourist trade based on casinos and inter-racial sex for white South Africans seeking respite from the 'Thou Shalt Not' of apartheid and Afrikaner puritanism.

Proponents of tourism stress its ability to bring much-needed foreign exchange earnings, international investment, improved infrastructure, employment, wildlife conservation and international understanding. Opponents argue that the proportion of foreign exchange earnings retained is small, perhaps 10 per cent, because tourism has a high import content from breakfast cereals to

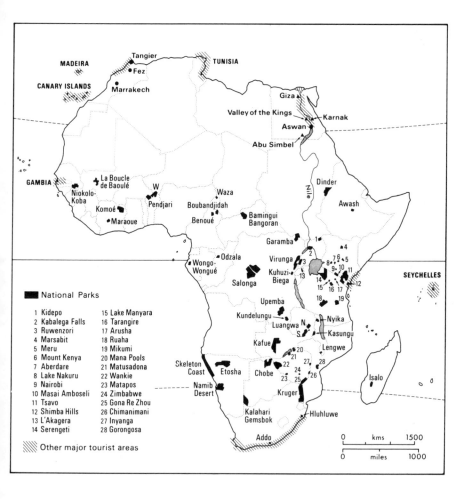

National Parks

1 Kidepo	15 Lake Manyara
2 Kabalega Falls	16 Tarangire
3 Ruwenzori	17 Arusha
4 Marsabit	18 Ruaha
5 Meru	19 Mikumi
6 Mount Kenya	20 Mana Pools
7 Aberdare	21 Matusadona
8 Lake Nakuru	22 Wankie
9 Nairobi	23 Matapos
10 Masai Amboseli	24 Zimbabwe
11 Tsavo	25 Gona Re Zhou
12 Shimba Hills	26 Chimanimani
13 L'Akagera	27 Inyanga
14 Serengeti	28 Gorongosa

Other major tourist areas

safari buses and hotel fittings. The international investment is for international consumption and home-based investment deprives some other sector of badly needed funds. Infrastructural development is specialized and of little benefit to the wider population; the jobs created are menial with management expensively bought in from outside. Conservation is often six safari buses grouped around one pride of lions with the only jumbo in sight a Boeing 747 overhead. The international understanding is more likely prostitution in the normal sense and also by putting 'on show' people who follow traditional ways of life. Africa will continue to develop tourism because it is one of the few options available but it is no easy highway to economic development.

149

47 Kenya

By virtue of its having large tracts of land more than 6000 ft (1829 m) above sea level Kenya was the only tropical colony to have a large white settler population. The White Highlands north-west of Nairobi were largely given over to white farming and cash crop cultivation. The alienation of this land caused a land shortage particularly among the Kikuyu on the eastern margin of the White Highlands. In the 1950s the Mau Mau troubles, for all the complexity of their origins, were essentially about land. They delayed independence in Kenya until December 1963 after Britain had released Jomo Kenyatta from detention, allegedly for involvement with Mau Mau, to become prime minister and later president.

The abused Kenyatta actually proved to be a most conservative leader much praised in the very newspapers in Britain which had once vilified him. Under him the Kenyan economy was capitalist free enterprise. Large amounts of investment were attracted and Nairobi mushroomed, an incongruously high-rise city in the wide open spaces of Africa. In the first two years of independence 14 per cent of white-held land passed to Africans, but most settlers remained in the country. In a broad agricultural base cash crops predominate led by coffee and tea. The tourist industry is the most highly developed in sub-Saharan Africa with fine modern hotels in Nairobi, along the Indian ocean coast and in the game parks where the lodges are oases of modern luxury. Investment has also been made in the industrial sector mainly at Nairobi and Mombasa the port of entry.

The tourist trade was one of many imbalances within the East African Community (EAC) and contributed to its demise. A typical East African safari holiday-maker would fly into Nairobi, spend some days based there with excursions to the adjacent Nairobi National Park and perhaps to a park such as Nakuru in the Rift Valley with its lake of 2 million flamingoes. Then a quick dash across the Tanzanian border to the Ngorongoro Crater and Serengeti. A fleeting glimpse of Kilimanjaro for the fortunate *en route* via Moshi and Voi for the Kenyan beach hotels between Mombasa and Malindi. Finally a few days for shopping in Nairobi before the flight home. Despite having the outstanding wildlife parks Tanzania received a very small proportion of such a trade. In frustration Tanzania built a new international airport at Arusha and in 1977 closed the Kenya border. It signalled the end of the EAC although there were of course many other contributory factors.

The end of the EAC hit Kenya badly and gone is the growth impetus helped also by world recession and the collapse of commodity prices. But what has also

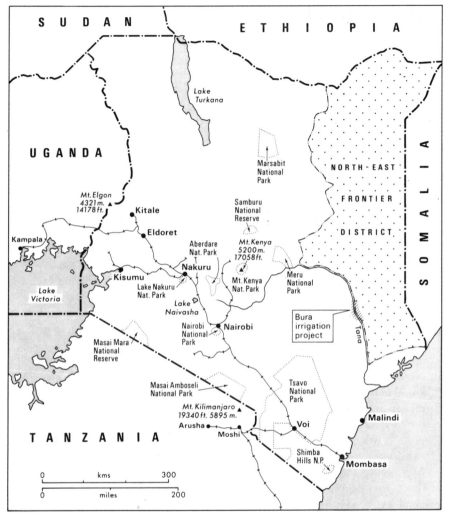

resurfaced is the land problem. The north and east of Kenya is arid with little potential. Cultivable land is in short supply and rapid population growth is putting severe pressure on existing land. The large US$200 million Bura irrigation scheme on the Tana river was aimed at ameliorating the problem. In early 1983 it was well behind schedule with escalating costs putting its whole viability at risk. With it would go many hopes which perhaps had always been forlorn. The bad times in Kenya provoked a serious attempted *coup d'état* in 1982. As at independence, as in the 1950s, the fundamental problem of Kenya is land.

48 Tanzania

Before independence in 1961 Julius Nyerere offered to delay even an event of that significance for Tanganyika in the interests of east African unity. In 1977 he closed the border between Tanzania and Kenya and so, in effect, brought the East African Community to an end. The disillusionment of Nyerere between 1961 and 1977 grew out of the inability of Kenya, Uganda and Tanzania to plan their co-operative development. Some stresses are inevitable in any community of nations. They are more likely to arise if there is no unifying ideology and they are less likely to be coped with because of a lack of political will. In east Africa it was worse than this because Kenya and Tanzania actually came to hold conflicting ideologies. This was not evident in 1961 and there was every hope that some common aim could be found once the absorbing issues of independence in the three territories had been resolved.

Tanzania covers a vast area, sparsely populated, but with areas of high population density on rich agricultural land notably on the southern slopes of Kilimanjaro and the Mwanza district south of Lake Victoria. There are some important cash crops, sisal west of Tanga, cotton in the Mwanza district, cashew nuts along the south coast and pyrethrum in the south-west. There is only one important mine, the Williamson diamond mine, one of the largest diamond pipes ever discovered. Other minerals are known to exist, including huge quantities of low-grade coal in the south-west, but are not worked. Tanzania is essentially a rural, agricultural country with plenty of land but needful of improvements in the rural sector. This is where Nyerere placed the emphasis in development plans. A new African socialism was born and western development economists wondered at the concept of *ujamaa*. Nyerere kindly wrote books to explain it. In Africa concentrate on rural development, rural settlements, rural infrastructure, rural water supply, rural co-operative marketing, rural self-help, rural communities. It was the sort of development which had to be planned as a co-operative enterprise. It was very different from the *laissez-faire* approach to economic development of Kenya. These differences spilt over into the EAC.

The economic geography of east Africa is such that a *laissez-faire* approach was bound to benefit Kenya to the detriment of Tanzania and Uganda. Nairobi, near the geographical centre, had been built up by the British into the economic hub of east Africa with good infrastructure and excellent communications. Outside investment if left to its own devices would gravitate towards Nairobi. To achieve balanced regional growth adequate mechanisms had to be devised to encourage or direct industry away from the centre, and where this was not

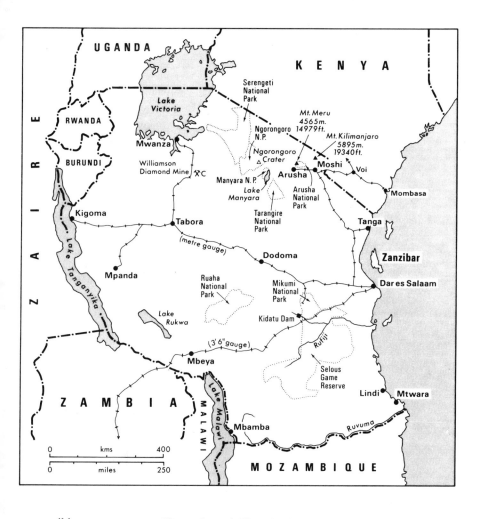

possible to compensate Tanzania and Uganda for the uneven distribution. Effective mechanisms were not found and so an important nail was put in the EAC coffin. There were other problems, not least Nyerere's unwillingness to deal with Amin in Uganda after the 1971 *coup* which came at a time when, although the EAC was already in some difficulty, Uganda and Tanzania were moving closely in step. There was also at that time the prospect of Zambia joining the EAC which would have shifted the centre of gravity towards Tanzania. For all the ideological differences Tanzania and Kenya have remained close together on the GDP per capita league table, neither improving its lot relative to other African states in the post-independence period.

49 Urbanization

In a continent where the vast majority of people are rural-dwellers it may seem strange that many of the social problems are associated with urbanization. In fact it follows, because over much of Africa urbanization is a recent phenomenon and many of the problems arise from the over-rapid growth of towns and the urban sector often at the expense of the rural.

Pre-colonial Africa was also pre-industrial and what towns existed then were essentially pre-industrial. There were the administrative centres of kingdoms and empires from Cairo to Bulawayo. There were trading towns at crossroads of commerce such as Gao and Timbuctoo on the southern fringe of the Sahara commanding routes in virtually all directions. In Yoruba-land the agricultural towns were of a different tradition. South of the Sahara the degree of urbanization was minimal.

Colonialism introduced the administrative capital, usually small in itself but a nucleus for powerful growth. It also brought ports to handle imperial trade, and most doubled as colonial capitals. Any significant settler population brought with it the urban tradition to found Salisbury (Harare), Nairobi and Windhoek while large mining areas developed associated towns from Kimberley to Johannesburg to Broken Hill (Kabwe) to Elisabethville (Lubumbashi) to Ndola. These various colonial implants attracted Africans from rural areas, either drawn in spontaneously or pulled in deliberately by the imposition of rural taxes by the colonial power. In most colonial towns influx was carefully controlled. The town itself was carefully planned and laid out in quite distinctive forms. Even in colonial times urban growth was often very great. Bulawayo grew from 29,000 in 1936 to 124,000 in 1951, Abidjan from 18,000 in 1933 to 119,000 in 1955.

With independence the move to towns increased. Many colonial curbs were removed, more urban-based jobs were created and the town became the place where it was all happening. Much of the increase was to the capital city and cities like Abidjan grew faster than ever before, by an estimated 11 per cent a year since independence to take it past the 1 million mark. But other centres grew too, although in much of Africa the primate city dominates.

The attraction of towns outstripped the towns' ability to cope with the inflow of people: services such as houses and basic utilities of water, electricity and sewerage could not be expanded fast enough. The overgrown African 'location' of Soweto (*South Western Townships*) in 1981 could boast only 10 per cent of its houses served by electricity. Jobs did not materialize as employment opportunities also failed to keep pace with the inflow. The response has not been to stem

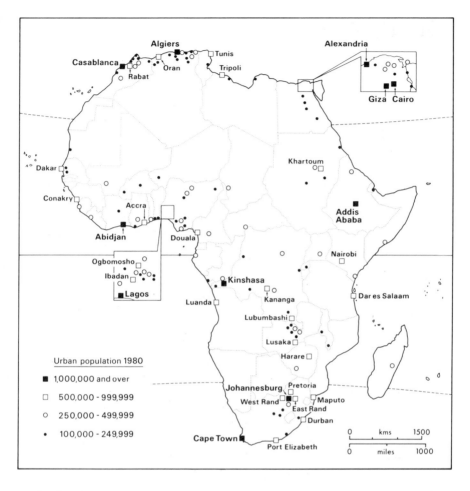

Urban population 1980

- ■ 1,000,000 and over
- □ 500,000 - 999,999
- ○ 250,000 - 499,999
- • 100,000 - 249,999

the flow but for want of houses, shanty towns; for want of jobs, an informal sector.

Continued urban growth causes problems. Urban congestion slows down economic development in the city while at the same time draining the potential for economic development in the countryside. In many towns there are genuine health hazards and serious deprivation resulting in disease and epidemics. But towns with mass unemployment also breed political discontent by the frustration of expectations often bred through inappropriate education. Already expressing himself in soaring crime rates the unemployed, underfed, deprived but somewhat educated African urban-dweller could become a major destabilizing influence in a continent that cries out for political stability.

50 Capital cities

With due allowance for the unreliability of basic statistics, African capital cities may be characterized as being usually primate cities, very large relative to other cities, large in absolute terms, very fast growing and faster growing than other cities. All but five African capital cities are the largest urban centres in their countries. The exceptions are Porto Novo (Benin) ranked 2, Yaoundé (Cameroon) 2, Lilongwe (Malawi) 2, Rabat (Morocco) 2, and Pretoria (South Africa) 4. (Pretoria is the administrative capital of South Africa, Cape Town is the legislative capital and Bloemfontein the judicial capital.)

The African capital city is often the *only* major urban centre in a state and is frequently many times greater in population than the second-ranking city. The following capital cities appear to be at least eight times larger than the next largest urban centre: Luanda (Angola), Bujumbura (Burundi), Bangui (CAR), Djibouti (Djibouti), Conakry (Guinea), Bissau (Guinea-Bissau), Abidjan (Ivory Coast), Maseru (Lesotho), Bamako (Mali), Maputo (Mozambique), Kigali (Rwanda) and Mogadishu (Somalia).

Many capital cities are large in absolute terms. At least six have populations of a million or more: Algiers, Cairo, Addis Ababa, Abidjan, Lagos and Kinshasa. Only in the least populous states are the capital cities of less than 50,000 population: Gaborone (Botswana), Praia (Cape Verde Islands), Moroni (Comoros), Malabo (Equatorial Guinea), Sao Tomé (St Thomas and Prince), Victoria (Seychelles) and Mbabane (Swaziland).

Capital cities are almost invariably the fastest growing cities in African states. Cities such as Yaoundé (Cameroon), Libreville (Gabon), Abidjan (Ivory Coast), Monravia (Liberia), Niamey (Niger), Lomé (Togo), Kampala (Uganda), Kinshasa (Zaire) and Lusaka (Zambia), all well established at independence, have apparently increased their population by more than five times since the late 1950s. Even in South Africa, where the rate of urban growth is deliberately depressed, Pretoria is the fastest growing large city. In five states where the capital is now the largest city, it was not so at the time of independence. Those cities are: Gaborone (Botswana), Nouakchott (Mauritania), Khartoum (Sudan), Ouagadougou (Burkina Faso) and Lusaka (Zambia).

In many cases the phenomenal rate of growth of capital cities is partly explained by changes affecting statistics, boundary adjustments or just unreliable enumeration. But the major part of the growth of individual capital cities derives from the singular attractiveness of these cities as places of employment, modernity and political power for they often perform a multitude of functions.

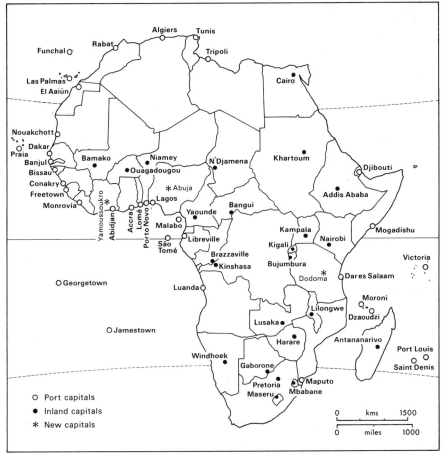

Algiers
Tunis
Funchal○
Rabat
Tripoli
Las Palmas○
El Aaiún
Cairo
Nouakchott○
Dakar
Praia
Banjul○
Bissau○
Bamako
Niamey
N'Djamena
Khartoum
Conakry○
Ouagadougou
Djibouti
Freetown
Abuja
Addis Ababa
Monrovia
Lagos
Yamoussoukro
Bangui
Abidjan
Accra
Lomé
Porto Novo
Yaounde
Malabo
Libreville
Kampala
Mogadishu
São Tomé
Kigali
Nairobi
Brazzaville
Bujumbura
Victoria
Kinshasa
Dodoma
Dar es Salaam
○Georgetown
Luanda○
Moroni
Lilongwe
Dzaoudzi
○Jamestown
Lusaka
Antananarivo
Port Louis
Harare
Saint Denis
Windhoek
Gaborone
Pretoria
Maputo
Maseru
Mbabane

○ Port capitals
● Inland capitals
* New capitals

0   kms   1500
0   miles   1000

Not only political capital, but also port and industrial commercial communications, educational and cultural centre.

Such overwhelming concentration is, in most cases, part of the colonial
inheritance. Colonial capitals, the seats of alien governments, were often located
just within the colony, at the point giving best access to the metropolitan
country. Hence along the west African coast, the seaboard states, without
exception, have port capital cities from Dakar to Lagos. In all, twenty-eight of
fifty-one African capital cities are ports, a very high proportion considering that
fourteen states are land-locked. Only Yaoundé, Brazzaville, Cairo, Addis Ababa,
Nairobi, Antananarivo, Pretoria, Khartoum and Kinshasa are non-seaport
capitals of seaboard states. Most of them have a special reason for so being – they
were not colonial creations.

157

A city that was colonial capital and chief port inevitably accumulated other functions and irresistible attractiveness, even where hot humid coastal climates and high incidence of disease were counterbalancing forces. The transformation from colonial capital to national capital accelerates growth as the concentration of functions is reinforced by the addition of the newly acquired instruments and symbols of international status and nationhood. The political function of the capital city in the newly independent state is a virile growth force. A seat of government immediately surrounds itself with the seemingly endless personnel of legislative and administrative bureaucracy, political parties and diplomatic representation. Secondary and tertiary growths mushroom especially with post-independence relaxation of colonially imposed influx-control.

Where *new* capitals were created at independence such as Nouakchott (Mauritania) and Gaborone (Botswana) they have forged ahead to become the largest urban centres, virtually from scratch, on the basis, originally, of only the political function. In countries of predominantly rural economic activity the political/administrative factor is dominant in the process of urbanization. In cities where the political function is one of many, as at Lagos or Maputo, over-concentration of urban growth leads to chronic congestion and inefficiency.

The marginal location of the colonial capital not only adds the basic function of a port to the capital city but also leaves this concentration of modern sector development remote from the geographical centre of the state. Many African capital cities could not be more geographically marginal as, for example, Lagos near one corner of the roughly square Nigeria, or Lomé at the corner of a very long and narrow, rectangular Togo. Even in some land-locked states the capital city is at or near one frontier, often at a point most accessible to the former metropolitan power, as at Bangui (CAR), Maseru (Lesotho) and N'djamena (Chad). Hot, steamy, but nearest to Cape Town and London, Livingstone was the colonial capital of Northern Rhodesia (Zambia) until higher, cooler, healthier and more central Lusaka was chosen as a new capital in 1931.

The process of economic development which is usually closely associated with the multifunctional capital city is not helped by the marginal location of most African capitals. Spread effects have far to travel, lines of communication are long and tenuous, some regions are incredibly remote. Nor is national unity, a prime concern in so many African states, well served by geographical remoteness.

The imbalance created by the all-attractive, multifunctional, peripherally located capital city has long been recognized, along with the positive remedial policy option of harnessing the virility of the political capital function to stimulate growth and development in more backward, more central regions. The dynamic capital city force can be relocated in a way a port or mineral-based urban complex never can be. But Africa has few Brasilias; Nouakchott and Gaborone, already mentioned, are not really in that category, both being created at the time of independence and both having geographically marginal locations.

The only full post-independence new capital city to have been completed in Africa is Lilongwe in land-locked, dependent, conservative Malawi. The decision to relocate the capital was taken in 1968 but it was not until 1975 that Lilongwe became the capital in succession to Zomba. Lilongwe is 180 miles (290 km) north of Zomba near the geographical centre and in the widest part of the elongated state. It enjoys good communications by tarred roads and rail and is 85 miles (135 km) from the lake shore. The development of Lilongwe was planned and carried out with substantial financial and technical assistance from South Africa. With a population of about 120,000 it is successfully contributing to a redistribution of economic development away from the Blantyre region in the extreme south.

Tanzania has decided to move its capital from the port of Dar es Salaam, to inland Dodoma where the Tanganyika railway crosses the 'Great North Road', 288 rail miles (460 km) west of Dar es Salaam, 267 road miles (427 km) south of Arusha. A long-established district and provincial administrative headquarters Dodoma is in a poorly developed region once famous for the groundnuts scheme fiasco. The cost of creating a new capital is considerable, not least because of the need to modernize the old routes which converge at Dodoma. It will be some time before the seat of government is relocated.

In 1976 Nigeria similarly decided to relocate its capital from the port of Lagos over 400 miles (650 km) inland to Abuja in a newly created Federal Capital Territory. The new federal capital will help ease the chronic congestion of Lagos and, located in the middle belt of Nigeria, it is also designed to contribute to national unity. Ambitious and costly plans include major communications improvements. Abuja was formally opened in 1982 but transfer of the capital city function will take some time.

In early 1983 the mayor of Abidjan suggested that Yamoussoukro become capital of the Ivory Coast, because of the familiar problems of congestion at Abidjan. Yamoussoukro commended itself not just because of its location but because it was the birthplace of President Felix Houphouët-Boigny. The mayor added that he was not being sycophantic in his suggestion.

The inheritance of the colonial capital city has had a harmful effect on many an African state. That few have so far taken positive action to relocate their capital is perhaps not surprising given the cost and necessary time-span of any such project. Advantages apparently clear in theory are not easily demonstrated in practice. In many states there is no viable alternative location and for others relocation would simply not be appropriate. Nevertheless, the developments unfolding in Tanzania and Nigeria will be carefully scrutinized in other African states to see what can be gained from following their examples.

51 Transport

Transport development in Africa has three distinct, if overlapping, phases: pre-colonial, colonial and post-colonial. However, most models of transport development in Africa are basically colonial in concept and so forfeit historical accuracy and current relevance. They also pay little attention to the fact that routes, especially those involving heavy capital investment, are developed with a specific goal in mind. Roads and railways are not built aimlessly across an isotropic surface through an apparently empty interior. Such models lack a logical dynamic and display weaknesses, enhanced by uncritical reception and dissemination, which lead to fundamental misconceptions about African transport development.

Before colonial times there were rich agricultural areas in Africa, concentrations of population, towns and cities and worked mineral deposits. People moved between such places along well-defined routes carrying trade goods over considerable distances. On the southern edge of the Sahara Timbuctoo and Gao stood at crossroads of trade. Across the Sahara came Mediterranean products and from the South came gold, ivory and slaves. Trans-Saharan and savanna routes long predated European exploration. To reach Timbuctoo Laing took caravan routes across the desert from Tripoli, while Caille obtained passage on a boat sailing down the Niger to return via the caravan route to Morocco.

The route from Bagamoyo to Lake Tanganyika was not hacked out by Burton and Speke, but was an old Arab trade route, in a sense colonial as it was developed to exploit ivory and slaves, but certainly pre-European. Kampala–Mengo long predated the arrival of Speke and Grant, and Zimbabwe traded with Sofala before the Portuguese sailed around the Cape. Pre-colonial Africa was patently not an empty continent.

When the Europeans came they established trading posts on the coast and, by offering higher prices for gold, ivory and slaves, contributed greatly to the decline of savanna market centres such as Timbuctoo. Early European traders did not venture far into the interior, being content to trade through African middlemen. But when they did it was usually to pre-existing African towns, often for military purposes. In Ghana the British, under Sir Garnet Wolseley, moved from the coast to attack Kumasi, the political capital of the Ashanti Kingdom. Wolseley built a military road from Accra to Kumasi, a route later followed by the railway built by the British colonial administration in 1923. In Nigeria British penetration was also to predetermined points, to pre-existing African cities such as Ibadan and Benin and later to Kano and Sokoto. Colonial

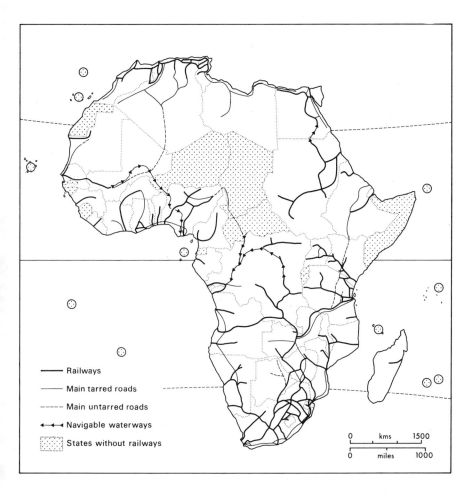

Railways
Main tarred roads
Main untarred roads
Navigable waterways
States without railways

| 0 | kms | 1500 |
| 0 | miles | 1000 |

transport routes were built from colonial ports to pre-colonial places and were
not developed in a virgin wilderness.

In southern Africa the colonial phase may be usefully divided into pre-
industrial and industrial, the latter dating from 1870 and the discovery of
diamonds at Kimberley. Pre-industrial colonial transport was mainly the ox-
wagon, a leisurely but effective means of travel from the ports to the few inland
centres. Accounts of such travel survive in sources as well known as
Livingstone's *Missionary Travels* (1857). The interior had little to attract
investment in any transport except ox-wagons which were adequate for carrying
the wool, hides and ivory produced. Penetration by railway was discouraged by
the outward-facing Great Escarpment and, in the south-west, the ranges of the

Cape Fold Mountains also parallel to the coast. By 1870 there were just 69 miles (110 km) of railways in South Africa, mainly linking Cape Town with Stellenbosch, Paarl and Wellington across the Cape Flats.

The discovery of four large diamond 'pipes' within a radius of 2 miles (3 km) at the heart of the subcontinent between September 1870 and June 1871 transformed transport development in southern Africa. The Cape Government took over existing private railways and under regional political pressure built lines towards Kimberley simultaneously from Cape Town, Port Elizabeth and East London. A new 'Cape Gauge' of 3 ft 6 in (1.065 m) was adopted to ease the engineering and financial problems of breaching the mountains but it was not until November 1885 that the railway reached Kimberley simultaneously from Cape Town and Port Elizabeth via De Aar junction.

In 1886 the Witwatersrand gold-fields were discovered, also localized and deep in the interior. Although a railway had been built to Ladysmith from Durban the first line to reach Johannesburg was an extension of the Cape line via Bloemfontein. Construction over the high veld was easier and cheaper than climbing the escarpment but the Natal line was also held at the Transvaal border to allow completion of the Transvaal's own direct line from Lourenço Marques (Maputo). The Cape–Bloemfontein line had been allowed to enter the Transvaal only after considerable political and financial pressure by Rhodes on Kruger.

From 1890 Rhodesia (Zimbabwe) became the next node. Although the direct Beira route was the looked-for means of rail access, the Matabele campaign of 1896 and severe rinderpest, which disrupted ox-wagon transport, led to the urgent mile-a-day extension of the spinal railway from Mafeking to Bulawayo, completed in November 1897. The Beira line, struggling through swamp and then over rugged escarpment, was completed to Salisbury (Harare) by 1900.

Farther north Broken Hill (Kabwe) and Katanga (Shaba) became new attractions reached by extension of the spinal railway in 1905 and 1910 respectively. The all-Belgian line from Port Francqui (Ilebo) was completed in 1926 in advance of the Benguela railway from Lobito (1928).

In 1915 the South African military campaign against the Germans in South-West Africa led to the Cape network being connected from De Aar to the German system built from the two ports of Luderitz and Swakopmund (later extended to Walvis Bay).

Southern Africa has by far the largest single rail network in Africa, over 20,000 route miles (32,000 km) in twelve different countries at the Cape gauge. The densest part of the network is in the richest country, South Africa which has over 13,500 route miles (21,560 km). The rail network does not merely serve important mineral-based nodes but also encourages development between nodes. Hence the concentration of economic development along the Durban–Johannesburg corridor, the Harare–Bulawayo axis and the Zambian 'line of rail'. Originally a colonial creation designed to facilitate mineral exploitation and to strengthen political domination, this rail network today provides South Africa with the means of maintaining economic and political hegemony over neighbouring states despite important post-independence railways built specifically to help break that dominance.

Post-colonial or independent transport development began in 1894 when the Transvaal's direct link with Lourenço Marques was built in an attempt to escape British domination. In 1955 Rhodesia opened a direct route to Lourenço Marques to maintain economic independence from South Africa, but when in 1975 Mozambique became independent Rhodesia quickly completed its direct rail link with South Africa having delayed doing so for almost fifty years. The most spectacular post-colonial railway in Africa is the 1050 mile (1680 km), Cape gauge, Tanzania–Zambia railway (TAZARA) from Zambia to Dar es Salaam, completed by the Chinese in 1975. It was planned specifically to help Zambia escape the economic and political clutches of Rhodesia and South Africa. Less ambitious but also built to give alternative access to the sea is the rail link between Malawi and Nacala. These lines reflect the fact that the decisions to build them were taken in independent African capital cities. They are not lines likely to have been built by colonial powers.

In East Africa three colonial lines from the ports of Mombasa, Tanga and Dar es Salaam were joined to form a single network at a metre gauge. The original lines were built for strategic colonial reasons to Lake Victoria and Uganda, to the rich agricultural area near Mount Kilimanjaro and to Lakes Tanganyika and Victoria. The first two were joined in 1916 by South African forces under General Smuts fresh from linking the Cape–South West African systems. The final link deliberately to make a single network significantly came after independence in 1964.

Elsewhere in Africa, except the Maghreb where a lateral line runs from Marakesh to Tunis, the railways are essentially colonial: short lines from the coast inland to mines, larger towns or rich agricultural areas with no lateral links. Three of them, from Dakar, Abidjan and Djibouti, do cross international boundaries. In Liberia and the Guinea the individual lines are of different gauge, making any lateral linkage difficult. Post-colonial additions have also extended some railways into remote areas to assist regional development, as the line to Maiduguri in north-eastern Nigeria and to Packwach in Uganda.

Ten territories on mainland Africa have no railways at all. Road building has gained momentum in the post-colonial period, but most trunk roads merely duplicate routes already served by rail, often from ports to the African interior. This reflects the continuing pattern of African trade which remains mainly with industrialized countries outside the continent with little intra-African trade development. The slow progress of the long-mooted trans-African highway

163

project illustrates the lack of urgency felt in Africa for such links. The subject of a resolution by the Council of Ministers of the ECA in 1971, the Trans-African Highway Authority was formally inaugurated no less than ten years later. Planned to run from Lagos to Mombasa it takes advantage of pre-existing roads for much of its distance but the central section through Cameroon, CAR and Zaire is very far from complete.

If Africa is ever going to free itself from a world trading system where it occupies a dependent role it must begin to develop an international continental infrastructure capable of promoting alternative trading patterns. Intra-African trade can only be expanded when the means for carrying on that trade are in place. Organizations such as SADCC have recognized the importance of transport and communications in their attempt to break away from dependence on white South Africa. The lesson is the same when applied to dependence on the continental African scale.

E The South

52 Interdependence in southern Africa

South Africa is by far the most powerful state in southern Africa in both economic and military terms. This strength is based on an incredibly rich resource base which has attracted enormous foreign investment and encouraged the growth of secondary and tertiary industries. By any economic indicator South Africa dwarfs its neighbours and under normal political conditions they would be in the dependent relationship of periphery to core. This relationship is made even less tolerable for the neighbouring states because, with the exception of Namibia, they are independent black African states politically opposed to South Africa's white-minority government which is intent on retaining political power through the system loosely known as apartheid. The South African government has long seen economic and, when necessary, military domination of the neighbouring states as a necessary part of its overall strategy for retaining power. The neighbouring states would all like to be free to develop independently and have joined together as the Southern Africa Development Co-ordination Conference (SADCC) to plan how they might do just that collectively. They first came together as 'front-line' states to press for political independence in Zimbabwe and although they are individually motivated to achieve economic independence from South Africa it is their political detestation and fear of that regime which fires their collective will.

Economic interdependence in southern Africa is not new. Most mining enterprises in the rest of southern Africa were the financial and technical satellites of the South African mining houses. The mines brought the railway which was an extension of the South African network. 'Web of steel' aptly describes the way in which the countries to the north have been enmeshed in South Africa's rail network. The mines in South Africa itself have always been hungry for labour and have recruited throughout southern Africa, in the past as far afield as Tanganyika and Angola. South Africa has been a source of manufactured goods often able to undercut many overseas supplies in price if not always in quality. Since 1910 there has been a customs union between South Africa and the three former High Commission Territories of Botswana, Lesotho and Swaziland which was renegotiated in 1970. These links are all long-standing but remain part of the interrelationships of southern Africa today.

The efficiency of South Africa and the relative inefficiency of its neighbours in running railways and harbours, mean that these countries frequently turn to South Africa for help with their own systems and for passage of imports and exports. South African locomotives work in Zambia, South Africans help run

SADCC States

Ports and railway network

- - - - - projected railways

Luanda
Lobito
Walvis Bay
Luderitz
Saldanha Bay
Cape Town
Port Elizabeth
East London
Durban
Richards Bay
Maputo
Beira
Nacala
Dar es Salaam

Customs Union

NAMIBIA
BOTSWANA
RSA
SWAZILAND
LESOTHO

RSA major external investments

Cunene
Cabora Bassa
Lilongwe

Migrant labour into RSA 1980

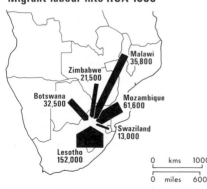

Malawi 35,800
Zimbabwe 21,500
Botswana 32,500
Mozambique 61,600
Swaziland 13,000
Lesotho 152,000

0   kms   1000
0   miles   600

RSA manpower 1980

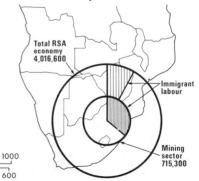

Total RSA economy 4,016,600
Immigrant labour
Mining sector 715,300

the port of Maputo, they service locomotives from Mozambique and help plan Swaziland railway developments. A large proportion of Zambian imports are still routed through South Africa which had the capacity to rail, for example, 450,000 tons of maize to Zambia in 1979 and to take in fertilizer for Zambia which congested Dar es Salaam could not handle. The SADCC states, realizing the importance of transport, have given it priority but there is still too much emphasis on new construction rather than the efficient operation of existing facilities. The 'helpful neighbour' stance of South Africa is alleged to mask a determination to see that transport in the SADCC states does not work, if necessary by force. The continued closure of the Benguela railway is caused by South African-backed UNITA forces in Angola and the sabotage of the Beira–Harare line in Mozambique in 1982 was also by South African-backed rebels, the MNR.

Since the wind of change has been blowing through southern Africa, South Africa has adopted an apparently Janus-like stance, on the one hand aiming to prevent or delay independence by propping up colonial settler regimes in Angola, Mozambique and Zimbabwe and by using military force as in Angola and Namibia and, on the other hand, co-operating to aid development in some SADCC states. The contradiction is more apparent than real because the aid is aimed at creating interdependencies which make it more difficult for those states to take action hostile to South Africa. The renegotiated customs union of 1970 is generous to Botswana, Lesotho and Swaziland but leaves them dependent on South Africa rather than British grants-in-aid, their former means of financial viability. Malawi is the only black African state to have full diplomatic relations with South Africa, the quid pro quo for which is South African aid, notably the planning, financing and construction of the new capital city of Lilongwe. A large proportion of Malawi's imports are from South Africa and over 35,000 Malawians are migrant workers in South Africa. The Cabora Bassa hydroelectric project in Mozambique largely financed and built by South Africans was completed on schedule in 1975 despite being in an area subject to FRELIMO attacks. During the Rhodesian crisis supplies of electricity to South Africa were uninterrupted although the transmission lines passed through the Patriotic Front's war zone. Over 50,000 Mozambicans work in South Africa which continues to pay a proportion of their earnings direct to the Mozambique government in gold.

Completely surrounded by South Africa, Lesotho is the most dependent neighbour. Over 150,000 Basuto are migrant workers in South Africa and the Lesotho economy probably could not survive any major decrease. Yet the South African mining sector, by far the most dependent on foreign migrant workers, is reducing that dependence by increasing productivity through mechanization and automation. Lesotho's vulnerability on another count was effectively

A Constellation of States

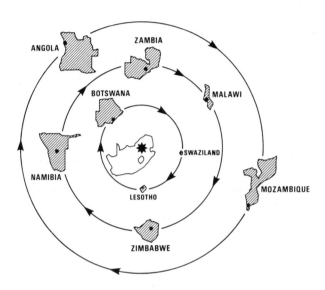

Development Co-ordination

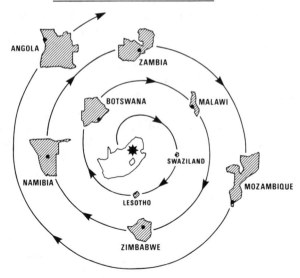

demonstrated in December 1982 when the South Africa Defence Force raided Maseru killing thirty ANC exiles and twelve Lesotho nationals.

The South African government is frank in its perception of its relationship with its neighbours. Its vision of a 'constellation of states' is proclaimed widely despite the fact that the implied static relationship does nothing for the aspirations of the SADCC states and must be ideologically unacceptable to them.

Nevertheless in March 1984 a major step towards the South African aim of political and economic domination of the sub-continent was taken when P. W. Botha and Samora Machel of Mozambique signed the Nkomati Accord, a non-aggression pact to which was added a series of agreements for mutual co-operation between their two countries. The need of Mozambique to seek a humiliating accommodation with South Africa reflected the ravages of drought and cyclone on a shaky agriculture and added to the military successes of the South African-backed MNR dissidents. The Accord was widely seen as a diplomatic triumph for South Africa. It confirmed South African ascendancy in the sub-continent and also helped secure South Africa internally by preventing Mozambique from being used as a springboard for guerilla attacks on the Republic by the ANC. At the same time it was revealed that a similar pact had earlier (1982) been signed between South Africa and Swaziland, and it became evident that other countries bordering South Africa were under intense diplomatic pressure from Pretoria to come to similar formal agreements. On the strength of the apparent success of his peace offensive (or offensive peace) in southern Africa Mr Botha was able to visit west European capitals in a bold attempt to end South Africa's political isolation. Unfortunately for him European leaders chose to emphasize their continuing concern about internal conditions within South Africa, in particular the unrelenting policy of re-settlement and forced migration. In early 1985 the South African government announced changes even to this policy but another storm of international protest broke on the shooting dead of nineteen blacks near Uitenhage on, of all days, the twenty-fifth anniversary of the killing of sixty-nine blacks at Sharpeville. Also in March 1985 the Nkomati Accord came under pressure from an unexpected quarter, the MNR, until then regarded as South Africa's lap-dogs. Their effective guerilla campaign against the Mozambique government continued with outside support to the embarrassment of the South Africans who had agreed to call them off.

53 Inside the laager

In 1948 the (Afrikaner) National Party came to power in South Africa, has remained in government ever since and seems unlikely to lose the support of the white-only electorate. A narrow, nationalistic, right-wing party, it stood for *Baaskaap*, keeping the blacks in their place. For its first ten years in office the party used every possible device systematically to eliminate all effective opposition and to consolidate its position. Then Dr H.F. Verwoerd succeeded to the premiership and, over eight years until his assassination in 1966, put South Africa on a new course. In 1961 after a referendum Verwoerd led South Africa to a republic outside the British Commonwealth and so ended the Anglo-Boer war. But above all Verwoerd was the chief architect of a new racial ideology, *apartheid*, Afrikanerdom's blueprint for survival. The Promotion of the Bantu Self-Government Act of 1959 provided the basis for the future evolution of 'separate development', 'Bantu homelands', and 'multinational development'. The act anticipated African homelands gaining *separate* independence, possibly to form a South African commonwealth with South Africa at its core. Afrikaners in government have striven for this ideal because they believed in Verwoerd when he declared that the alternative was domination by the black majority; for a minority to rule it must divide the majority.

Perhaps apartheid began when Jan van Riebeeck the first governor of the Cape, planted a hedge of thorn and wild almonds to separate Dutch from Khoi-Khoi (Hottentots). Certainly from 1652 whites acquired increasingly more land in South Africa. Some land was unoccupied, some was apparently unoccupied, some was purchased from African chiefs who had no concept of buying and selling land because it was vested in the tribe and transactions in land were totally outside their social experience. Much land was also acquired by right of conquest and Africans were forced into the poorer parts of areas they had once occupied.

When the Union of South Africa was created in 1910 land for Africans was a political issue. The Natives Land Act of 1913 scheduled 22.5 million acres (9.1 million ha) as 'Native Reserves' for exclusive African occupation, but outside which no African could acquire land. The 'Scheduled Areas' amounted to 7.3 per cent of the area of South Africa at a time when Africans accounted for 67.3 per cent of the population. The inadequacy was evident, so the Beaumont Commission was set up to achieve a 'final settlement'. In 1916 it recommended the 'release' of a further 16.8 million acres (6.8 million ha) along with extensive consolidation of the highly fragmented existing African lands. The resultant bill failed to emerge from parliamentary committee in 1917 and the proposals were never implemented.

The land question was finally settled in Afrikaner eyes in 1936 when the Native Trust and Land Act allowed for an additional 'quota' of 15.3 million acres (6.2 million ha) to be released for black occupation. The Act remains the yardstick for the division of land in South Africa although in 1980 about 1.222 million acres (0.495 million ha) remained to be acquired under it. When fully implemented 13.8 per cent of land in South Africa will be in black areas. In 1980 black population in South Africa stood at 20.22 million of a total population of 28.02 million, about 72.2 per cent.

From Verwoerd's blueprint multinational development evolved. Black 'homelands' were identified, some were given internal self-government and some moved on to 'independence', a status shared by the Transkei (1976), Boputhatswana (1977), Venda (1979) and the Ciskei (1981). Their 'independence' is not recognized beyond South Africa, yet pressure is being exerted on other black homelands to accept 'independence'.

Homelands emphasize tribalism with home language the main criterion for division, but not rigorously so, for both the Transkei and Ciskei are Xhosa speaking. The homelands are home to less than half the blacks in South Africa. In 1980 47.7 per cent of blacks lived in their appropriate homeland, 52.3 per cent elsewhere, mainly in white South Africa. The original tribal areas were very much larger and in the case of the South Sotho and Swazi adjoin the independent states of Lesotho and Swaziland. In 1982 the South African government set up a deal with Swaziland whereby the 0.74 million Swazi who are citizens of South Africa would become Swaziland citizens in return for land ceded by South Africa to Swaziland including Tongaland. Land-locked Swaziland would have gained access to the sea and South Africa would have 'lost' some blacks and gained an extension of the Swazi buffer against infiltrations from Mozambique. The deal fell through because Tongaland is part of the Zulu rather than the Swazi homeland and contains the grave of the Zulu King Dingane.

Blacks resident in white South Africa are regarded as *de jure* citizens of their language-group homeland. This status is imposed even on blacks born in white South Africa and resident there all their lives. It makes them 'black aliens' liable to deportation and they lose any rights possessed by black South Africans. The policy also imposes on the 'independent' homeland a total population it could not possibly support.

The homelands are at best mere fragments of areas traditionally occupied by the tribal groups. The amount of land available in total is inadequate even for the *de facto* population. The *de facto* population density of the black areas in 1980 was 171 per square mile (66 per sq. km), higher than any continental African

1913
Bantu Land Act:
scheduled areas

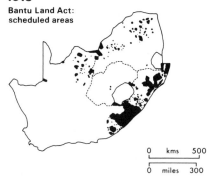

1916
Beaumont Commission
Proposals:
never implemented

```
0      kms     500
0      miles   300
```

1936
Bantu Trust and Land Act:
scheduled areas and
released areas

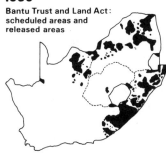

1975
Black Homelands:
actual black areas

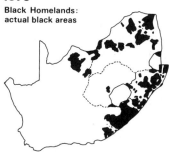

1975
Black Homelands:
consolidation proposals
not yet implemented

1982
Black Homelands:
'Independent'
homelands

Venda

Bophuthatswana

Ciskei   Transkei

country except Rwanda. Many homelands are oddly shaped fragments of land spattered across the map of South Africa. In 1975 there were ninety-six separate pieces of black land exclusive of so-called 'black spots' in white areas. Kwazulu comprised forty-four separate units of land. 'Independent' Boputhatswana has one parcel of land which is over 150 miles (250 km) from the nearest of the others. Consolidation proposals tabled in 1975 aim to reduce the parcels of land to thirty-four, much the same as Beaumont suggested in 1916, once the 'black spots' are eliminated.

'Black spots' have been systematically cleared. Over half a million people have been relocated under this programme. In Natal alone it has been estimated that 189 black spots remain to be dealt with, involving a quarter of a million people. In 1970–9 115,636 persons were moved as part of urban relocation. The 1975 consolidation proposals will relocate about 1 million people. In 1982 The Black Sash Organization estimated that in the period 1960–80 about 3 million people had been forced to move. Relocation and resettlement on this scale in pursuit of multinational development ideology is one of the greatest causes of misery and human suffering in South Africa.

The black homelands are residual economic backwaters into which blacks were pushed away from main rail and road routes, from major mineral resources and the richest agricultural land. No major dam, power installation, irrigation scheme nor factory sullies the fragmented face of the homelands. With a *de facto* 38 per cent of South African population the homelands share less than 3 per cent of South African GDP. In the homelands GDP per capita ranged from R 88 to R 132 a year in 1981 compared with the South African national average, including the homelands, of R 2550 a year. Much homeland income is derived from migrant and commuter workers in South Africa. Remittances from such workers in 1976 totalled R 2206 million. In 1981 migrant and commuter workers from Kwazulu outnumbered workers in Kwazulu by 12 to 1. It is clearly difficult to claim any sort of economic viability for such territories.

The homelands, including the 'independents', are heavily dependent on South Africa. Apart from remittances, the homelands received R 194 million from South Africa in 1979–80 while R 136 million went to the Transkei and Boputhatswana. But the South African government has consistently fallen behind in implementing its own policy, be it investment and job creation following the Tomlinson Commission (1955), or land acquisition following the Trust and Land Act (1936) or consolidation following Beaumont (1916). None of the targets set at these various, now distant, dates has yet been met. The commitment to the ideal is less than wholehearted where it costs money.

The homelands are reservoirs of cheap labour essential for industrial South Africa. They are also a vital means of reducing the numerical odds against whites in white South Africa, a role that can be enhanced with their economic development. The homelands therefore have important economic and political functions in relation to the grand design of a constellation of states. They form an inner ring of dependent satellites, a sort of fragmented meteorite belt.

The homelands are the periphery of South Africa, urban blacks are at the core. White South Africa has yet to find a way to deal with this group so that they will not present a threat to white hegemony. In 1984 an election of Coloureds and Indians to separate houses (of Representatives and Delegates respectively) aimed, by constitutional juggling, to transform the political line up from white versus non-white to black versus non-black. The exercise which had won white approval through a referendum was less than convincing because fewer than 20 per cent of potential voters participated. The elections also sparked off fresh urban unrest among blacks who were offered no parallel form of representation. During the first three months of 1985 on average one black per day was shot dead by South African police culminating in the death of nineteen blacks at Uitenhage on 21 March. Sooner or later urban blacks will also have to be accommodated, because they are essential to white South African prosperity and are the long-term threat to white power. The white right wing strongly opposes any constitutional concessions and is a brake on reform but is also a convenient excuse for the lack of progress of a government whose real desire for radical change seldom matches its own propaganda. A conservative bureaucracy and a police force firmly wedded to the use of the sjambok and live bullets are also important impediments to change. Nevertheless changes are taking place in South Africa, by no means are they all cosmetic and most emanate from the government. Whether they will proceed quickly enough and far enough to satisfy non-white and international demands is doubtful. For example the promised repeal of parts of the 'Immorality Act' to allow 'mixed' marriages will be deemed significant only when racial classification itself is dropped. The Afrikaner is fighting for cultural survival as well as to maintain a position of economic or class privilege. Survival depends on the possession of total political power. Abrogation of power without cast-iron guarantees is seen to be suicidal, and there are no cast-iron guarantees and never can be.

54 Strategic minerals in southern Africa

The strategic importance of southern Africa lies in its mineral wealth and the Cape sea route. Both are potentially threatened by racial conflict arising from white South African determination to stand against the tide of black African independence and to preserve their economic and political hegemony over the region. White South Africa maintains that the threat comes not from their stance but from world communism working through black liberation movements to destabilize the region and so deprive the west of vital minerals.

The mineral wealth of southern Africa is enormous, varied and widely distributed. The region is the world's largest single source of gold, diamonds, cobalt, platinum, chrome, copper, vanadium, manganese and possibly uranium. It also has vast resources of iron-ore, coal, phosphates and asbestos, and lesser quantities of lead, zinc, nickel and tin. Most of these are vital to modern industry and some especially so to 'high-tech' industries. For some, such as platinum, chrome and vanadium there is no other significant source available to the west.

Mining has been established in the region since the discovery of the first of the Kimberley diamond pipes in 1870. The profits from Kimberley were used to open up the Witwatersrand gold-fields from 1886 which in turn became the financial, technical and managerial springboard for subsequent mining enterprises farther north in the Rhodesias (Zimbabwe and Zambia) from 1890 and Katanga (Shaba) from 1910, as well as elsewhere in South Africa. Mining houses such as the Anglo-American Corporation are active throughout the region. They are backed by a sophisticated infrastructure of the spinal railway which was extended stage by stage from one newly activated mining node to another; lateral railway 'ribs' constructed to ports which were built to handle the bulk of minerals extracted from the interior; a network of modern roads and expanding electricity grids from the great dams on the Zambezi and Orange rivers.

It is argued that all this is safeguarded by white South Africa. That the greater part of southern Africa which is already black-majority ruled is also maintained technically, and kept in line politically, by white South Africa. Zambia and Mozambique are not very good at running railways and ports so that at best the end of white-minority rule in South Africa, and the inevitable exodus of already scarce skilled labour, would see severe technical disruptions. At worst supplies would cease altogether. But the mineral-producing black states are tied to a world trading system which is a treadmill they, including Soviet-supported

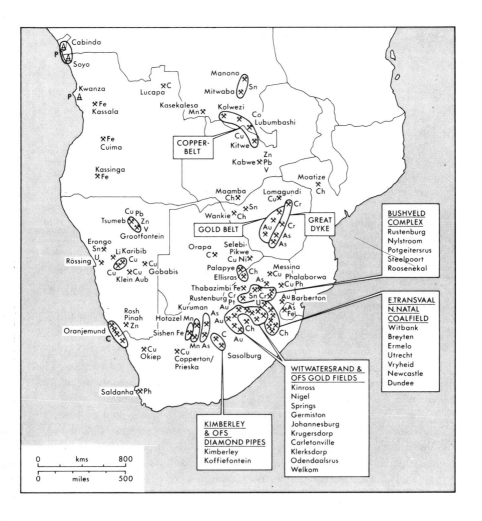

Angola, cannot get off. Western companies dealing with black governments of any political persuasion hold the trump cards. All they require is stability, under whatever ideological banner, and the long-term prospect for such stability might lie with majority rather than minority rule. The mining companies are not so much alarmed at the prospect of the demise of the apartheid state but of the threatened violence of its death throes, for they are quite capable of dealing with black Africa and the Soviet Union even when the two are lined up together, which is not very often. For the African it is a case of 'a plague on all your houses', mining companies, white South Africans and Soviets, for none help him get maximum benefit from the mineral wealth of southern Africa.

55 Namibia: Africa's last colony

It could be argued that the scramble for Africa began when Bismarck extended imperial protection to the activities of the Bremen trader Franz Luderitz in South West Africa (Namibia) including the small harbour the Portuguese had called Angra Pequena, known for the past century as Luderitz Bay. Today Namibia is the last colony in Africa and it has all the ingredients necessary for a long and painful decolonization process. It has a proportionately large white population of about 110,000 or about 10 per cent, and a small African population of about 1 million concentrated in the northern tenth of the country. Namibia has enormous mineral wealth exploited vigorously by large multinational corporations and, above all, neighbouring South Africa as the colonial power. Once treated as an integral part of South Africa, Namibia is now part of South Africa's own defence strategy against the encroachment of black-majority rule. Namibia is the last sangar before the laager itself.

South West Africa was ruthlessly subjugated by the Germans, but in 1915 Botha and Smuts made short work of defeating the German forces there. In 1920 it became a League of Nations mandated territory entrusted to South Africa. Many German settlers stayed on, their numbers augmented by Afrikaners. The great mineral wealth of the country began to be revealed, notably the alluvial diamonds along the beaches north of the mouth of the Orange river.

In 1945 the mandate was transferred to the UN but when the UN sought to exercise its rights in Namibia South Africa challenged its status in a long battle through the International Court. Meanwhile South Africa ruled the territory *de facto* as a fifth province partly to help solve its constitutional battle at home over parliamentary representation for non-whites. In 1971 the International Court eventually advised against South African 'occupation' of Namibia. The struggle entered a new phase in 1975 with Angolan independence.

The SWAPO liberation movement became more effective, having a wider base to operate from. The South African policy of *détente* with its neighbours collapsed after the abortive invasion of Angola in 1975 and pressure in the UN and from the west increased. The Turnhalle constitutional conference, excluding SWAPO, was set up in 1975 to seek an 'internal solution'. Dissolved in 1977 a majority of its participants formed the Democratic Turnhalle Alliance (DTA) backed by South Africa. Under pressure from the Western Contact Group elections were agreed for Namibia in 1978 but lost credibility when SWAPO boycotted them. DTA was elected despite little support from the white electorate but in effect Namibia continued to be run by a South African

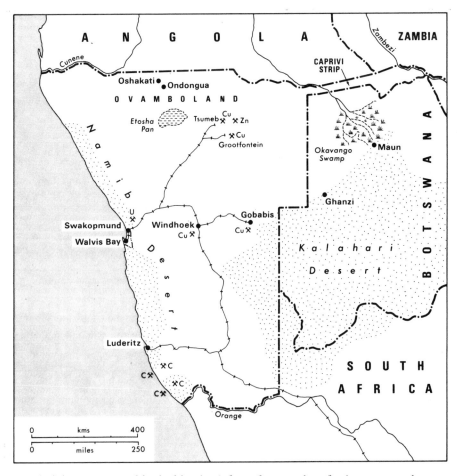

administrator-general backed by the defence force, and no further progress has been made towards independence. Meanwhile mining of Namibia's rich resources continues unabated.

Walvis Bay and several small offshore islands were originally British. In 1883 they passed to the Cape and subsequently to South Africa and were separate from German territory. In 1915 Walvis Bay became and has remained the main port of Namibia, whilst the former guano islands carry important fishing rights. In 1977 when independence for Namibia seemed imminent all were returned to the administration of the Cape Province of South Africa. The Namibia/South Africa boundary runs along the north bank of the Orange river so denying water rights to Namibia. These minutiae of political geography could feature prominently in future independence negotiations.

Appendices

56 Chronology of African independence

State	Date of Independence	Colonial Power	Notes
Ethiopia	Ancient	—	Italian occupation 1936–41.
Liberia	26.7.1847	—	Private colony 1822–47.
South Africa	31.5.1910	Britain	(*Suid Afrika*) Union of four colonies, Cape Colony, Natal, Orange River Colony (*Oranje Vrij Staat*) and Transvaal (*Zuid Afrikaansche Republiek*), the last two of which had been independent republics to 31.5.1902. The Union became republic outside the British Commonwealth 31.5.1961. White minority rule. Unrecognized 'independent' homelands: Transkei 26.10.1976 Boputhatswana 6.12.1977 Venda 13.9.1979 Ciskei 4.12.1981
Egypt	28.2.1922	Britain	United with Syria as United Arab Republic (UAR) from 1.2.1958 to 28.9.1961. Federated with Kingdom of Yemen from 8.3.1958 to 26.12.1961. Name of UAR retained by Egypt until 2.9.1971.
Libya	24.12.1951	Italy	British (Tripolitania and Cyrenaica) and French (Fezzan) administration 1943–51.
Ethiopia (Eritrea)	11.9.1952	Italy	British administration 1941–52. Federation of Eritrea and Ethiopia 1952. Full union 14.11.1962.
Ethiopia (Ogaden)	1955		Italian occupation 1936–41. British administration 1941–55.
Sudan	1.1.1956	Britain Egypt	Anglo-Egyptian condominium.
Morocco	2.3.1956	France	(*Maroc*)
Tunisia	20.3.1956	France	(*Tunisie*)
Morocco (part)	7.4.1956	Spain	(*Marruecos*) Spanish northern zone.
Morocco (part)	29.10.1956		International zone (Tangier).

State	Date of Independence	Colonial Power	Notes
Ghana	6.3.1957	Britain	(Gold Coast) including British Togoland (UN trust), part of former German colony of Togo.
Morocco (part)	27.4.1958	Spain	(*Marruecos*) Spanish southern zone.
Guinea	2.10.1958	France	(*Guinée Française*)
Cameroon	1.1.1960	France	(*Cameroun*) UN trust. Larger part of former German colony of *Kamerun*.
Togo	27.4.1960	France	UN trust. Larger part of former German colony of Togo.
Senegal	20.6.1960 (20.8.1960)	France	Independent initially as 'Federation of Mali' with former French Soudan (Mali). Federation broke up after two months. Joined with the Gambia as Confederation of Senegambia from 1.1.1982.
Mali	20.6.1960 (22.9.1960)	France	(*Soudan Français*) Independent initially as 'Federation of Mali' with Senegal. Federation broke up after two months.
Madagascar	26.6.1960	France	(Malagasy; *République Malagache*)
Zaire	30.6.1960	Belgium	Congo Free State (*Etat Indépendant du Congo*) 2.5.1885 to 18.11.1908 when it became the Belgian Congo (*Congo Belge, Belgisch Congo*). Name changed from Congo on 27.10.1971.
Somalia	1.7.1960	Italy Britain	UN trust. Union of two colonies. British Somaliland independent prior to union from 26.6.1960.
Benin	1.8.1960	France	Name changed from Dahomey on 30.11.1975.
Niger	3.8.1960	France	
Burkina Faso	5.8.1960	France	Name changed from Upper Volta (*Haute Volta*) on 4.8.1984.
Ivory Coast	7.8.1960	France	(*Côte d'Ivoire*)
Chad	11.8.1960	France	(*Tchad*)
Central African Republic (CAR)	13.8.1960	France	(*Obangui-Chari, Republique Centrafricaine*) Central African Empire from 4.12.1976 to 20.9.1979.
Congo (Brazzaville)	15.8.1960	France	(*Moyen Congo*)
Gabon	17.8.1960	France	
Nigeria	1.10.1960	Britain	
Mauritania	28.11.1960	France	(*Mauretanie*)
Sierra Leone	27.4.1961	Britain	

State	Date of Independence	Colonial Power	Notes
Nigeria (British Cameroon North)	1.6.1961	Britain	UN trust. Part of former German colony of *Kamerun*. Plebiscite 11/12.2.1961.
Cameroon (British Cameroon South)	1.10.1961	Britain	UN trust. Part of former German colony of *Kamerun*. Plebiscite) 11/12.2.1961. Union with Cameroon as United Republic of Cameroon.
Tanzania	9.12.1961	Britain	(Tanganyika) UN trust. Greater part of former German colony of *Deutsche Ostafrika*. Name changed to Tanzania following union with Zanzibar 27.4.1964.
Burundi	1.7.1962	Belgium	UN trust. Ruanda-Urundi, divided at independence, was smaller part of former German colony of *Deutsche Ostafrika*.
Rwanda	1.7.1962	Belgium	
Algeria	3.7.1962	France	(*Algérie*)
Uganda	9.10.1962	Britair	
Tanzania (Zanzibar)	10.12.1963	Britain	Union with Tanganyika as Tanzania 27.4.1964.
Kenya	12.12.1963	Britain	
Malawi	6.7.1964	Britain	(Nyasaland) Federated with Rhodesias 1.10.1953 to 31.12.1963.
Zambia	24.10.1964	Britain	(Northern Rhodesia) Federated with Nyasaland and Southern Rhodesia 1.10.1953 to 31.12.1963.
Gambia	18.2.1965	Britain	Joined with Senegal as Confederation Senegambia from 1.1.1982.
Botswana	30.9.1966	Britain	(Bechuanaland)
Lesotho	4.10.1966	Britain	(Basutoland)
Mauritius	12.3.1968	Britain	
Swaziland	6.9.1968	Britain	
Equatorial Guinea	12.10.1968	Spain	Comprises *Rio Muni* and *Macias Nguema Biyogo (Fernando Poo)*.
Morocco (Ifni)	30.6.1969	Spain	(*Territorio ae Ijni*)
Guinea-Bissau	10.9.1974	Portugal	*Guine-Bissau* formerly *Guine Portuguesa*.
Mozambique	25.6.1975	Portugal	(*Moçambique*)
Cape Verde	5.7.1975	Portugal	(*Cabo Verde*)
Comoros	6.7.1975	France	*Archipel des (Comores)* Excluding island of Mayotte which remains a French Overseas Territory (*Territoire d'Outre-Mer*).

State	Date of Independence	Colonial Power	Notes
St Thomas & Prince Islands	12.7.1975	Portugal	(*Sao Tomé e Principe*)
Angola	11.11.1975	Portugal	(Including Cabinda)
Western Sahara	28.2.1975	Spain	(*Rio de Oro* and *Seguit el Hamra*) on Spanish withdrawal seized by Morocco. Occupation disputed by POLISARIO, formed 10.5.1973.
Seychelles	26.6.1976	Britain	
Djibouti	27.6.1977	France	(*Territoire Française des Afars et des Issas* formerly *Côte Française des Somalis*)
Zimbabwe	18.4.1980	Britain	(Rhodesia, formerly Southern Rhodesia) UDI in effect from 11.11.1965 to 12.12.1979. Federated with Northern Rhodesia and Nyasaland 1.10.1953 to 31.12.1963.

Territories not independent

State		Colonial Power	Notes
Namibia		South Africa	(South West Africa) UN trust. Former German colony of *Deutsche Südwestafrika*. South Africa in dispute with UN.
Spanish North Africa		Spain	*Plazas de Soberania: Ceuta, Islas Chafarinas, Melilla, Penon de Velez de la Gomera, Penon de Alhucemas.* Small enclaves and islands on the north coast of Morocco.
Madeira		Portugal	(*Arquipelago da Madeira*)
Canary Islands		Spain	(*Islas Canarias*)
St Helena with Ascension and Tristan da Cunha		Britain	British Crown Colony
Socotra		Southern Yemen	
Mayotte		France	Island of Comoros Group. Overseas Territory of France.
Reunion		France	*Ile de la Réunion*, Overseas Department of France (*Département d'Outre-Mer*) (from 1946).
French Indian Ocean Islands		France	*Ile Europa, Ile Juan de Nova, Bassas da India, Iles Glorieuses, Ile Tromelin* (all near Madagascar).

57 States, capitals, changes of government and political leaders of post-colonial Africa

State	Capital		Dates			Leaders
			A	B	C	
Algeria	Algiers	P	1962			Ben Bella
					1965	*Boumedienne* (d)
				1979		*Chadli Bendjedid*
Angola	Luanda	P	1975			Neto (d)
				1979		Dos Santos
Benin	Porto Novo	P	1960			Maga
					1963	Ahomadegbe/Apithy
					1965	*Soglo*
					1967	*Alley*
					1969	*De Souza*
					1972	*Kerekou*
Botswana	Gaborone	L	1966			Khama (d)
				1980		Masire
Burkina Faso	Ouagadougou	L	1960			Yameogo
					1966	*Lamizana*
					1980	*Zerbo*
					1982	*Ouedraogo*
					1983	*Sankara*
Burundi	Bujumbura	L	1962			(Mwami) Mwambutse IV
					1966	(Mwami) Ntare V (e 1972)
					1966	*Micombero*
					1976	*Bagaza*
Cameroon	Yaoundé		1960			Ahidjo
				1982		Biya
Cape Verde	Praia	P	1975			Pereira
Central African Republic	Bangui	L	1960			Dacko
					1965	*Bokassa*
					1979	Dacko
					1981	*Kolingbo*
Chad	N'Djamena	L	1960			Tombalbaye (a)
					1975	*Malloum*
				1979		Goukouni Oueddei

State	Capital		Dates			Leaders
			A	B	C	
				1979		Choua
				1979		Goukouni Oueddei
					1982	Habré
Comoros	Moroni	P	1975			Solih
					1978	Abdallah
Congo	Brazzaville	—	1960			Youlou
					1963	Massamba-Debat (e)
					1968	*Ngouabi* (a)
					1977	*Yhombi-Opango*
				1979		*Sassou-Nguesso*
Djibouti	Djibouti	P	1977			Gouled
Egypt	Cairo	—	1922			
				1936		(King) Farouk
					1952	*Neguib*
				1954		*Nasser* (d)
				1970		*Sadat* (a)
				1981		*Mubarak*
Equatorial	Malabo	P	1968			Nguema (e)
Guinea					1979	*Mbasogo*
Ethiopia	Addis Ababa	—	Ancient			
				1930		(Emperor) Haile Selassie
					1974	*Aman Adom* (a)
				1974		*Teferi Banti* (e)
				1977		*Mengistu*
Gabon	Libreville	P	1960			M'Ba (d)
				1967		Bongo
Gambia	Banjul	P	1965			Jawara
Ghana	Accra	P	1957			Nkrumah
					1966	*Ankrah*
				1969		*Afrifa* (e 1979)
				1969		Busia
					1972	*Acheampong* (e 1979)
					1978	*Akuffo* (e 1979)
					1979	*Rawlings*
				1979		Limann
					1981	*Rawlings*
Guinea	Conakry	P	1958			Sekou Toure
				1984		Beavogui
					1984	*Conte*

State	Capital		A	B	C	Leaders
Guinea-Bissau	Bissau	P	1974			Luiz Cabral
					1980	*Vieira*
Ivory Coast	Abidjan	P				Houphouët-Boigny
Kenya	Nairobi	—	1963			Kenyatta (d)
				1978		Arap-Moi
Lesotho	Maseru	L	1966			(King) Moshoeshoe II/ Jonathan
					1970	Jonathan
Liberia	Monrovia	P	1847			
				1944		Tubman (d)
				1971		Tolbert (a)
					1980	*Doe*
Libya	Tripoli	P	1951			(King) Idris
					1969	*Gadafy*
Madagascar	Antananarivo		1960			Tsiranana
		—			1972	*Ramanantsoa*
				1975		*Ratsimandrava* (a)
				1975		*Anriamahazo*
				1975		*Ratsiraka*
Malawi	Lilongwe	L	1964			Banda
Mali	Bamako	L	1960			Keita
					1968	*Traore*
Mauritania	Nouakchott	P	1960			Ould Daddah
					1978	*Salek*
					1979	*Louly*
					1980	*Haidalla*
Mauritius	Port Louis	P	1968			Ramgoolam
				1982		Jugnauth
Morocco	Rabat	—	1956			(King) Mohammed V (d)
				1961		(King) Hassan II
Mozambique	Maputo	P	1975			Machel
Niger	Niamey	L	1960			Diori
					1974	*Kountche*
Nigeria	Lagos	P	1960			Balewa (a)
					1966	*Ironsi*
					1966	*Gowon*
					1975	*Murtala Muhammed* (a)
				1976		*Obasanjo*
				1979		Shehu Shagari
					1983	*Buhari*

188

State	Capital		A	B	C	Leaders
Rwanda	Kigali	L	1962			Kayibanda
					1973	*Habyrimana*
St Thomas & Prince Islands	Sao Tomé	P	1975			Da Costa
Senegal	Dakar	P	1960			Senghor
				1981		Diouf
Seychelles	Victoria	P	1976			Mancham
					1977	René
Sierra Leone	Freetown	P	1961			Milton Margai (d)
				1964		Albert Margai
					1967	*Juxon-Smith*
					1968	Stevens
Somalia	Mogadishu	P	1960			Shirmarke (a 1969)
				1964		Haji Hussein
				1967		Egal
					1969	*Siad Barre*
South Africa	Pretoria	—	1910			
				1948		Malan
				1954		Strijdom (d)
				1958		Verwoerd (a)
				1966		Vorster
				1978		Botha
Sudan	Khartoum	—	1956			Khalil
					1958	*Abboud*
					1964	Al-Khalifa
				1965		Mahgoub
				1966		Sadiq
					1969	*Nimeiri*
					1983	*Swareddahab*
Swaziland	Mbabane	L	1968			(King) Sobhuza II (d)
				1982		(Queen Regent) for (Prince) Makhosetive
Tanzania	Dar es Salaam	P	1961			Nyerere
Togo	Lomé	P	1960			Olympio (a)
					1963	Grunitzky
					1967	*Eyadema*
Tunisia	Tunis	P	1956			(Bey) Sidi Mohammed al-Amin/Borguiba
					1957	Borguiba

State	Capital		Dates			Leaders
			A	B	C	
Uganda	Kampala	L	1962			(Kabaka) Mutesa II/Obote
					1966	Obote
					1971	*Amin*
					1979	Lule
				1979		Binaisa
				1980		Obote
Zaire	Kinshasa	—	1960			Lumumba (e 1961)
					1960	*Mobutu*
				1961		Adoula
				1964		Tshombe
					1965	*Mobutu*
Zambia	Lusaka	L	1964			Kaunda
Zanzibar*	Zanzibar	P	1963			(Sultan) Abdullah bin Khalifa
					1964	Karume (a 1972)
Zimbabwe	Harare	L	1980			Mugabe

Notes: CAPITAL P – port capital city   L – land-locked state

DATES   A – independence   B – peaceful change of government   C – successful *coup d'état*

LEADERS Military leaders in italics
(a) assassinated   (d) died   (e) executed

*   Zanzibar joined with Tanganyika as Tanzania in April 1964

58   Area, population and GNP; population density, GNP per capita, GNP per capita growth rates and life expectancy

Country	Area (sq.km)	GNP (million US $ 1983)	Popul'n ('000 1983)	Persons per sq.km (1983)	GNP per capita (US $ 1983)	Growth rates (%) GNP per capita (1973-82)	Life expect. 1982
Algeria	2,381,741	49,450	20,569	8·6	2,400	2·4	57
Angola	1,246,700	*	8,206	6·6	*	*	43
Benin	112,622	1,110	3,809	33·8	290	2·7	48
Botswana	600,372	920	998	1·7	920	5·0	61
Burkina Faso	274,200	1,210	6,666	24·3	180	1·6	44
Burundi	27,834	1,050	4,466	160·5	240	*	47
Cameroon	475,442	7,640	9,562	20·1	800	4·6	53
Cape Verde	4,033	110	308	76·4	360	4·1	61
Central African R.	622,984	690	2,470	4·0	280	− 1·3	48
Chad	1,284,000	400	4,747	3·7	80	− 7·7	44
Comoros	2,400	136	378	157·5	340	0	48
Congo	342,000	2,180	1,768	5·2	1,230	3·6	60
Djibouti	22,733	*	399	17·6	*	*	50
Egypt	1,001,449	31,880	45,364	45·3	700	6·6	57
Equatorial Guinea	28,051	*	360	12·8	*	*	44
Ethiopia	1,221,900	4,860	33,908	27·7	140	0·7	47
Gabon	267,667	2,950	695	2·6	4,250	− 4·7	50
Gambia	11,295	200	697	62·0	290	− 0·8	36
Ghana	238,537	3,980	12,518	52·5	320	− 3·8	55
Guinea	254,857	1,740	5,831	22·9	300	0·5	38
Guinea-Bissau	36,125	150	866	24·0	180	− 2·1	38
Ivory Coast	322,463	6,730	9,294	28·8	720	1·1	47
Kenya	582,645	6,450	18,900	32·4	340	1·0	57
Lesotho	30,355	670	1,437	47·3	470	4·0	53
Liberia	111,369	990	2,090	18·8	470	− 0·9	54
Libya	1,759,540	25,100	3,344	1·9	7,500	0·3	57
Madagascar	687,041	2,730	9,435	13·7	290	− 2·5	48
Malawi	118,484	1,390	6,670	56·3	210	1·1	44
Mali	1,240,000	1,110	7,277	5·9	150	2·1	45
Mauritania	1,030,700	720	1,637	1·6	440	0·7	45
Mauritius	2,045	1,250	999	488·5	1,150	2·3	67

Country	Area (sq.km)	GNP (million US $ 1983)	Popul'n ('000 1983)	Persons per sq.km (1983)	GNP per capita (US $ 1983)	Growth rates (%) GNP per capita (1973–82)	Life expect. 1982
Morocco	446,550	15,620	20,801	46·6	750	2·1	52
Mozambique	783,030	*	13,345	17·0	*	*	51
Niger	1,267,000	1,460	6,057	4·8	240	2·8	45
Nigeria	923,768	71,030	93,642	101·4	760	− 0·7	50
Rwanda	26,338	1,540	5,720	217·2	270	2·3	46
St Thomas & Prince	964	30	103	106·8	310	1·4	62
Senegal	196,192	2,730	6,195	31·6	440	− 0·7	44
Seychelles	518	160	65	125·5	2,400	3·7	70
Sierra Leone	71,740	1,230	3,265	45·5	380	− 0·3	38
Somalia	637,657	1,140	4,641	7·3	250	1·9	39
South Africa	1,221,037	76,890	31,345	25·7	2,450	0·5	63
Sudan	2,505,813	8,420	20,807	8·3	400	3·5	47
Swaziland	17,363	610	688	39·6	890	0	55
Tanzania	945,087	4,880	20,410	21·6	240	0·1	52
Togo	56,000	790	2,847	50·8	280	0·4	47
Tunisia	164,150	8,860	6,846	41·7	1,290	4·1	61
Uganda	236,036	3,090	13,881	58·8	220	− 5·6	47
Zaire	2,354,409	5,050	31,627	13.4	160	− 4·2	50
Zambia	752,614	3,630	6,255	8·3	580	− 2·5	51
Zimbabwe	390,580	5,820	7,822	20·0	740	0·4	56
Namibia	824,292	1,920	1,088	1·3	1,760	1·8	60
Reunion	2,510	2,060	554	220·7	3,710	− 0·5	66
Total/average	30,165,232	*	523,672	17·4	*	*	*

Source: World Bank Atlas 1985   *Data not available

Other African territories

Country	Area (sq.km)	Popul'n ('000 1981)
Canary Islands	7,273	1,140
French Indian Ocean Islands	50	0
Madeira	796	270
Mayotte	374	50
St Helena & dependencies	396	10
Socotra	3,626	—
Spanish North Africa	36	170
Western Sahara	266,770	150
Total	30,444,553	525,462

Select bibliography

Abrahams, P. (1956) *A Wreath for Udomo*, London, Faber & Faber.

Achebe, C. (1958) *Things Fall Apart*, London, Heinemann.

Best, A. and de Blij, H. (1977) *African Survey*, New York, Wiley.

Carpenter, R. (1973) *Beyond the Pillars of Hercules*, London, Tandem. (First published by Delacorte Press in USA, 1966.)

Chaliand, G. (1982) *The Struggle for Africa: Conflict of the Great Powers*, London, Macmillan. (First published in France in 1980 as *L'Enjeu Africain*.)

Conrad, J. (1902) *The Heart of Darkness*, London, Dent.

Davidson, B. (1978) *Africa in Modern History*, London, Penguin.

Davidson, B. and Bronda, A. (1980) *Cross Roads in Africa*, Nottingham, Spokesman Books.

Denoon, D. (1972) *Southern Africa Since 1800*, London, Longman.

Dumont, R. (1966) *False Start in Africa*, London, André Deutsch. (First published in France in 1962 as *L'Afrique Noire est Mal Partie*.)

Dumont, R. and Mottin, M-F. (1983) *Stranglehold on Africa*, London, André Deutsch. (First published in France in 1980 as *L'Afrique Etranglée*.)

Environmental Development Action (1981) *Environment and Development in Africa*, Oxford, Pergamon.

Europa (annual) *Africa South of the Sahara*, London, Europa Publications.

Fage, J. (1958, 1978) *An Atlas of African History*, London, Arnold.

Gavshon, A. (1981) *Crisis in Africa: Battleground of East and West*, London, Penguin.

Gourou, P. (1953, 1958) *The Tropical World*, London, Longman. (First published in France as *Les Pays Tropicaux*.)

Green, R. *et al.* (eds) (1981) *Namibia: the Last Colony*, London, Longman.

Griffiths, J.F. (ed.) (1972) *Climates of Africa*, London, Elsevier.

Grove, A.T. (1970) *Africa South of the Sahara*, London, Oxford University Press.

Grove, A.T. and Klein, F.M.G. (1979) *Rural Africa*, Cambridge University Press.

Lord Hailey (1938) *An African Survey*, London, Oxford University Press.

Hanks, R.J. (1981) *The Cape Route: Imperiled Western Lifeline*, Cambridge, Mass., Institute for Foreign Policy Analysis.

Hodder, B.W. (1978) *Africa Today*, London, Methuen.

Hodgkin, T. (1956) *Nationalism in Colonial Africa*, London, Muller.

Hodgson, R.D. and Stoneman, E.A. (1968, second ed.) *The Changing Map of Africa*, Princeton, NJ, Van Nostrand.

Hopkins, A.G. (1973) *An Economic History of West Africa*, London, Longman.

Horrell, M. (ed.) (annual) *Survey of Race Relations in South Africa*, Johannesburg, South African Institute of Race Relations.

Huddleston, T. (1956) *Naught for Your Comfort*, London, Collins.

Johnson, R.W. (1977) *How Long Will South Africa Survive?* London, Macmillan.

Kaunda, K. (1966) *A Humanist in Africa*, London, Longman.

Keltie, J.S. (1893) *The Partition of Africa*, London, Stanford.

Kgarebe, A. (1981) *SADCC 2 – Maputo*, London, SADCC Liaison Committee.

Lanning, G. (1979) *Africa Undermined*, London, Pelican.

Leakey, R. and Lewin, R. (1977) *Origins*, London, Macdonald & Janes.

Legum, C. and Hodges, T. (1976) *After Angola: the War Over Southern Africa*, London, Rex Collings.

Lemon, A. (1976) *Apartheid*, Farnborough, Saxon House.

Livingstone, D. (1857) *Missionary Travels and Researches in South Africa*, London, John Murray.

Mabogunje, A. (1980) *The Development Process: a Spatial Perspective*, London, Hutchinson.

McMaster, D.N. (ed.) (1974) *Tourism in Africa*, Centre of African Studies, University of Edinburgh.

MacMillan, W.M. (1949) *Africa Emergent*, London, Penguin.

Mazrui, A.A. (1980) *The African Condition*, London, Heinemann.

Nkrumah, K. (1963) *Africa Must Unite*, London, Heinemann.

Nsekela, A.J. (ed.) (1981) *Southern Africa: Toward Economic Liberation*, London, Rex Collings.

Nyerere, J. (1966) *Ujamaa: Essays on Socialism*, Dar es Salaam, Oxford University Press.

Oliver, R. and Crowder, M. (eds) (1981) *The Cambridge Encyclopaedia of Africa*, Cambridge, Cambridge University Press.

Palmer, R. (1977) *Land and Racial Domination in Rhodesia*, London, Heinemann.

Pool, D. (1980) *Eritrea: Africa's Longest War*, London Anti-Slavery Society Human Rights Services, Report No. 3.

Prothero, R.M. (1972) *People and Land in Africa South of the Sahara*, London, Oxford University Press.

Reeves, A. (1960) *Shooting at Sharpeville*, London, Victor Gollancz.

Republic of South Africa (annual, from 1974) *South Africa: Official Yearbook of the Republic of South Africa*, Johannesburg, Chris van Rensburg Publications.

Rodney, W. (1972) *How Europe Underdeveloped Africa*, Dar es Salaam, Tanzania Publishing House.

Rogers, B. (1980, revised ed.) *Divide and Rule: South Africa's Bantustans*, London, International Defence and Aid Fund.

Schreiner, O. (1883) *The Story of an African Farm*, London, Hutchinson.

Selassie, B.H. (1980) *Conflict and Intervention in the Horn of Africa*, New York and London, Monthly Review Press.

Stanley, H.M. (1878) *Through the Dark Continent*, London, Sampson Low, Marston, Searle & Rivington.

Thomas, M.F. and Whittington, G.W. (1969) *Environment and Land Use in Africa*, London, Methuen.

Widstrand, C.G. (ed.) (1969) *African Boundary Problems*, Uppsala, Scandinavian Institute of African Studies.

World Bank (annual) *World Bank Atlas*, Washington DC, IBRD/WB.

Index